Detailed Healthy

Air Fryer Cookbook

100 Recipes

"Quick, Healthy, and Flavourful Meals for Every Occasion"

By Amelia Rose Garcia

TABLE OF CONTENT

Introducing "Air Fryer Magic: 100 Easy and Delicious Rec ipes," a gastronomic journey that will revolutionize the way you prepare and savor your favorite dishes.

Because it uses a fraction of the oil used in traditional frying met hods to produce crispy, tasty food, the air fryer has quickly beco me a cherished kitchen device..This book is your go-to resource for learning the art of air frying, whether you're a sea soned chef or a home cook searching for quick, healthful meals.T he Ascent of Air FryerThe popularity of air fryers is a revolution i n home cooking, not just a fad.

With good reason, the air fryer has won the hearts of millions of people all around the world since its debut.

With the help of hot air circulation,

This multifunctional equipment cooks food evenly and gives

it the perfect crispy finish without using a lot of oil.

You can thus enjoy the flavor of your favorite fried foods without feeling as guilty.One of the key advantages of air fryer cooking is its health benefits.

Large volumes of oil are frequently used for traditional frying tec hniques, which results in high fat and calorie content.

Conversely, air frying consumes up to 80% less oil, making it a h ealthier option.

Furthermore, the quick air circulation guarantees uniform cooki ng of the meal, retaining moisture and flavor and minimizing the requirement for additional fats.Why Opt for Air Frying?Better Co oking for Health:

As was previously noted, air frying drastically lowers the amoun t of oil required to get that ideal crispiness.

This implies that you can indulge in your favorite fried dishes wh ile consuming less fat and calories.

For people who wish to keep up a healthy lifestyle without comp romising flavor, it's a win-

win situation.Convenience: Air fryers are very easy to use.

Preset cooking features and user-

friendly controls are standard on most models, which simplify th e process of preparing a broad range of dishes.

The air fryer can easily handle any type of cooking, from a simple midweek supper to a lavish weekend feast.adaptability: The air f ryer's adaptability is among its most amazing features.

The air fryer can be used for everything from side dishes to dess erts, appetizers to main courses.

This book contains recipes for many delicious dishes,

including crispy chicken wings, savory veggies, exquisite seafood , and sweet desserts.Speed:

Air fryers are a great option for families and busy individuals bec -ause they cook food more quickly than traditional ovens.

Your food will be cooked to perfection in a fraction of the time it would take to prepare using traditional methods thanks to quick air circulation technology.

Easy cleanup: Using an air fryer makes cleaning up after coo king—an sometimes difficult task—much simpler.

The majority of air fryer trays and baskets are dishwasher safe, a nd the non-

stick coatings minimize food adhering, cutting down on cleaning time and effort.How to Begin Using Your Air FryerIt's important to familiarize oneself with the fundamentals of air frying before getting into the recipes.

To get you started and help you get the most out of your air fry,

Consider the following advice: Preheating your air fryer can assist guarantee even cooking, just like preheating an oven. It usually just takes a few minutes for an air fryer to reach the right temperature, so be sure to warm it before adding any food.

Don't Overcrowd:

Try not to pack the air fryer basket too full for optimal results. Serve your food in a single layer so that hot air can flow around each portion uniformly.

This will guarantee that your food cooks through thoroughly and crisps up to perfection.Shake It Up: To ensure an even crispiness for foods like fries or tiny veggies, shake the basket halfway through cooking.

By taking this easy step, you can make sure that the meal gets heated on all sides.Even while an air fryer uses a lot less oil, you can still improve the crispiness of your food by lightly misting it with oil.

For optimal results, coat the meal with a small bit of oil or use cooking spray.Try Different Temperatures and Times: Cooking times and temperatures vary depending on the meal.

Try new things and make adjustments based on your personal tastes without fear.

Although this book offers suggestions, you'll get the best results if you make your cuisine uniquely your own.What Is Included in For your convenience, "Air Fryer Magic: 100 Easy and Delicious Recipes" is broken up into sections that will help you quickly locate the exact recipe you're looking for.

Every category has a wide variety of foods to fit a variety of palates and nutritional needs.

This is a little peek at what to expect:

Breakfast Bonanza: Start your day with delicious breakfast options like fluffy air fryer pancakes, crispy bacon, and savory breakfast burritos. These recipes are designed to give you a nutritious and satisfying start to your morning.

Appetizers and Snacks: Whether you're hosting a party or craving a mid-day snack, this section has you covered. From crispy mozzarella sticks to spicy buffalo cauliflower bites, these appetizers are perfect for any occasion.

Main Courses: Discover a wide range of main course recipes that will satisfy every palate. Enjoy juicy air fryer chicken, tender beef, flavorful seafood, and vegetarian delights. Every recipe is designed to provide the most flavor with the least amount of work.

Side Dishes: Elevate your meals with an array of side dishes that complement any main course. From perfectly roasted vegetables to golden-brown fries, these side dishes are the ideal accompaniments to your favorite meals.

Desserts: Indulge your sweet tooth with delectable air fryer desserts. Try mouth-watering chocolate chip cookies, crispy churros, and even air-fried apple pie. These desserts are sure to impress and satisfy your cravings.

Healthy Options: This section has meals that are high in flavor b ut low in calories for individuals trying to stick to a healthy diet.

Global Flavors: Take your taste buds on a journey around the world with recipes inspired by international cuisines. From Italian-inspired arancini to Asian-style spring rolls, these recipes bring global flavors to your kitchen.

Kids' Favorites: Make mealtime fun and exciting for your little ones with recipes tailored to their tastes. Discover kid-friendly options like chicken tenders, mini pizzas, and cheesy stuffed mushrooms.

The Magic of Air Frying

At the heart of this book is the belief that cooking should be a joyful and creative experience. The air fryer, with its convenience and versatility, opens up a world of culinary possibilities. Whether you're a busy parent, a working professional, or someone who simply loves to cook, the air fryer can make your life easier and your meals more delicious.

Air frying is not just about replicating the taste and texture of fried foods; it's about exploring new flavors, experimenting with ingredients, and embracing a healthier way of cooking. It's about the magic that happens when hot air and a little bit of oil come together to create something truly special.

This book is meant to be your cooking partner, providing you wit h detailed directions, advice, and methods to help you master the art of air-frying.
To guarantee that you always get the greatest outcomes, each for mula has been painstakingly created and put through testing.
There are recipes that inspire and excite you whether you're a co oking beginner or expert.

Tips for Success

Read the Manual: Every air fryer model is different, so take the time to read the manual that comes with your appliance. Familiarize yourself with the settings, functions, and safety precautions to ensure optimal use.

Invest in Accessories: There are several accessories available that can enhance your air frying experience. Consider investing in a baking pan, a rack, or skewers designed for air fryers to expand your cooking possibilities.

Use Premium, Fresh Components: For best results, use premium, fresh components.
You may improve the taste and texture of your food by adding fresh veggies, meats, and herbs.

Season Well: Don't skimp on seasoning. Properly seasoned food can make a world of difference. Experiment with different spices, herbs, and marinades to find your perfect flavor combinations.

Keep an Eye on Your Food: Pay attention to your food as it cooks.
As opposed to traditional cooking methods, air fryers cook food faster, thus it's important to check the doneness to avoid overcooking.

Enjoy the Process: Cooking with an air fryer is meant to be fun and enjoyable. Don't be afraid to experiment, try new recipes, and make adjustments based on your preferences. The more you use your air fryer, the more confident and creative you'll become.

Conclusion

"Air Fryer Magic:

100 Easy and Delicious Recipes" is more than just a cookbook; it's an invitation to explore the endless possibilities-of-air-frying. This book is here to support you every step of the way, whether your goals are to eat tasty meals, make better choices, or simply save time in the kitchen.

Marsel Guardio, with his extensive culinary experience and passion for home cooking, has crafted this collection of recipes to inspire and delight. Every recipe aims to be easy to follow and use ingredients and methods that cooks of all skill levels can use. Remember that the charm of cooking is the satisfaction that com es from producing and serving delectable meals to the people yo u care about as you begin your air fryer adventure.
Now that your air fryer is turned on, assemble your supplies, and get readto discover the wonders of air cooking.

Happy cooking!

AIR FRYER COOKBOOK:RECIPES

CHICKEN RECIPES

1. CLASSIC AIR FRYER FRIED CHICKEN

INGREDIENTS:

- ❖ 4 chicken thighs, bone-in and skin-on
- ❖ 1 cup buttermilk
- ❖ 1 cup all-purpose flour
- ❖ 1 teaspoon paprika
- ❖ 1 teaspoon garlic powder
- ❖ 1 teaspoon onion powder
- ❖ 1/2 teaspoon salt
- ❖ 1/2 teaspoon black pepper
- ❖ Cooking spray

INSTRUCTIONS:

1. To marinate the chicken, put the thighs in a big dish and cover them with buttermilk. Make sure the chicken is immersed all the way. For optimal effects, cover and refrigerate for at least two hours, preferably overnight.
2. Get the coating ready:
3. In a small bowl, mix the flour, paprika, onion, garlic powders, salt, and pepper. Blend thoroughly.
4. Apply Coat to Chicken:
5. Take out each chicken thigh and let any extra buttermilk fall off. Gently press the seasoned flour mixture onto the

chicken to ensure it sticks. Toss away any additional flour.

6. Warm up the air fryer.
7. For around five minutes, preheat the air fryer to 360°F (182°C).
8. Prepare the chicken:
9. To avoid sticking the air fryer basket, lightly mist it with cooking spray. Place the coated chicken thighs in the basket in a single layer, and apply cooking spray to the chicken's tops.
10. Cook for 25 to 30 minutes at 360°F (182°C), turning the chicken halfway through. Finish the chicken until it's golden brown and 165°F (74°C).
11. Take a Break and Serve:
12. The chicken should rest for five minutes after taking it out of the air fryer before being served. By helping to move the liquids around, this keeps the chicken juicy.

NOTE:

➢ Before cooking, carefully spray the chicken with oil so as not to overcrowd the basket for extra crispy skin. You might have to cook in batches depending on your air fryer's size.
➢ Add cayenne pepper or spicy sauce to the buttermilk marinade for a spicier variation.

2. LEMON HERB CHICKEN BREASTS

INGREDIENTS:

- ❖ 2 boneless, skinless chicken breasts
- ❖ 2 tablespoons olive oil
- ❖ 2 tablespoons lemon juice
- ❖ 1 tablespoon lemon zest
- ❖ 2 cloves garlic, minced
- ❖ 1 teaspoon dried oregano
- ❖ 1 teaspoon dried thyme
- ❖ 1/2 teaspoon dried rosemary
- ❖ 1/2 teaspoon salt
- ❖ 1/4 teaspoon black pepper
- ❖ Fresh parsley, chopped (for garnish, optional)

INSTRUCTIONS:

1. Make the marinade:
2. Salt, pepper, oregano, thyme, rosemary, lemon juice, and zest should all be mixed together in a small bowl.
3. Marinate chicken. Put chicken breasts in a shallow dish or bag. Coat chicken evenly after marinating. Refrigerate the bag or dish for 30 minutes or 4 hours for better flavor.
4. Warm the air fryer: Preheat the air fryer for five minutes at 380°F (193°C).
5. Let excess marinade drip off chicken breasts before grilling. Single-layer the chicken breasts in the air fryer basket. Use cooking spray gently to brown.

6. Stir once as you simmer at 380°F/193°C for 15–20 minutes. A golden brown chicken with an internal temperature of 1 is done.
7. Rest and Serve: Let the air-fried chicken breasts settle for five minutes before slicing. If desired, add fresh parsley.

NOTE:

➢ Make sure the chicken breasts are uniformly thick for even frying. If they are excessively thick, think about slicing them in half horizontally or pounding them until they are uniformly thick.
➢ This marinade can also be used for drumsticks or chicken thighs. As necessary, modify the cooking time.

3, SPICY BUFFALO CHICKEN WINGS

INGREDIENTS:

- ❖ 2 pounds chicken wings, separated into flats and drumettes
- ❖ 1 tablespoon olive oil
- ❖ 1/2 teaspoon garlic powder
- ❖ 1/2 teaspoon onion powder
- ❖ 1/2 teaspoon smoked paprika
- ❖ 1/4 teaspoon cayenne pepper
- ❖ 1/2 teaspoon salt
- ❖ 1/4 teaspoon black pepper

For the Buffalo Sauce:

- ❖ 1/2 cup hot sauce (e.g., Frank's RedHot)
- ❖ 1/4 cup unsalted butter
- ❖ 1 tablespoon white vinegar
- ❖ 1/2 teaspoon garlic powder
- ❖ 1/2 teaspoon onion powder

INSTRUCTIONS:

1. Wing preparation:
2. Use paper towels to dry chicken wings. In a big bowl, rub the wings with olive oil, smoked paprika, onion, garlic, cayenne, salt, and black pepper.
3. Warm the air fryer.

4. Heating the air fryer to 360°F (182°C)
5. takes five minutes.
6. Wing prep:
7. Single-layer wings in air fryer basket. Batch cooking reduces crowding. Air-fry the wings for 25–30 minutes at 360°F (182°C) until crispy and 165°F (74°C) inside. Shake the basket halfway through.
8. Prepare
9. Buffalo Sauce.
10. Make the sauce while the wings cook. Butter melts in a small pot over medium heat. Add onion powder, garlic powder, white vinegar, and spicy sauce after melting. Stir until heated and blended.
11. Coat the Wings: Place cooked wings in a large dish. Toss wings in buffalo sauce to coat.

Serve:

➤ Add celery sticks and your preferred dipping sauce (blue cheese or ranch) to the hot wings.

NOTE:

➤ Before cooking, pat the wings dry and refrigerate uncovered for a few hours for extra crispy wings. This makes the skin crispier and helps remove moisture.
➤ Depending on how hot you like your food, you can change the amount of cayenne pepper in the seasoning or hot sauce.

4. HONEY GARLIC CHICKEN THIGHS

INGREDIENTS:

- ❖ 4 bone-in, skinless chicken thighs
- ❖ 2 tablespoons honey
- ❖ 2 tablespoons soy sauce
- ❖ 2 tablespoons rice vinegar
- ❖ 3 cloves garlic, minced
- ❖ 1 tablespoon olive oil
- ❖ 1/2 teaspoon ground ginger
- ❖ 1/4 teaspoon red pepper flakes
- ❖ 1/2 teaspoon salt
- ❖ 1/4 teaspoon black peppers
- ❖ chopped green onions and sesame seeds

INSTRUCTION:

1. Get the marinade ready:
2. In a bowl, mix honey, soy sauce, rice vinegar, ground ginger, olive oil, minced garlic, red pepper flakes (if used), salt, and black pepper.
3. Put the thighs in a shallow dish or resealable plastic bag to marinate the chicken. After pouring the marinade over the chicken, ensure it is evenly coated. Refrigerate for at least 30 minutes, or up to 4 hours for more flavor, after sealing the bag or covering the dish.
4. Heat the Air Fryer: Set the air fryer's temperature to 380°F (193°C) for five minutes.

5. Lift the chicken thighs from the marinade and discard the excess before cooking. Place the chicken thighs in an air fryer basket in a single layer. A little layer of frying spray helps them brown.
6. Turn the chicken halfway through cooking it at 380°F/193°C for 20–25 minutes until golden brown and 165°F (74°C). If the marinade caramelizes, it may adhere to the chicken.
7. Rest the chicken after air-frying before garnishing and serving. Add green onions and sesame seeds if preferred.

NOTE:

➢ Reduce skillet marinade before serving for a deeper glaze. Brush the chicken with the thickened marinade from a saucepan.
➢ Dry chicken thighs before marinating for stickiness. If the air fryer is complete, cook the thighs in batches for even cooking.

5. PARMESAN CRUSTED CHICKEN TENDERS

INGREDIENTS:

- ❖ 1 pound chicken tenders (about 8-10 tenders)
- ❖ 1/2 cup all-purpose flour
- ❖ 2 large eggs
- ❖ 1 cup grated Parmesan cheese
- ❖ 1 cup panko breadcrumbs
- ❖ 1 teaspoon dried oregano
- ❖ 1 teaspoon garlic powder
- ❖ 1/2 teaspoon paprika
- ❖ 1/2 teaspoon salt
- ❖ 1/4 teaspoon black pepper
- ❖ Cooking spray

INSTRUCTIONS:

1. Arrange three shallow bowls to serve as the breading stations. Put the flour in the first bowl. Beat the eggs in the other bowl. Parmesan cheese, panko breadcrumbs, paprika, oregano, garlic powder, salt, and black pepper should all be combined in the third bowl.
2. Bread the Chicken: Shake off excess flour after dredging each tender chicken in flour.
3. Shake off any excess egg by dipping the floured chicken tender into the beaten egg mixture.
4. Press the Parmesan breadcrumb mixture onto the chicken tender, ensuring it coats the entire surface evenly.

5. The air fryer should be preheated for five minutes to 400°F (204°C).
6. Cook the tenders of chicken:
7. The air fryer basket should hold one layer of breaded chicken tenders. To crisp the tops, lightly spray with cooking spray.
8. Turn the chicken tenders over after 10 to 12 minutes at 400°F (204°C). You should be able to tell they are done when they are golden brown and 165°F (74°C).

Serve:

Take the chicken tenders from the air fryer and let them rest for a few minutes before arranging them on a platter. Serve with your preferred dipping sauce, like honey mustard or marinara.

NOTE:

➢ Cooking spray should be used on the tenders, and the basket should not be overcrowded for extra crispy tenders. Cook, if necessary, in batches.
➢ For an extra cheesy touch, sprinkle the chicken tenders with a little amount of freshly grated Parmesan during the last few minutes of cooking.

6. BBQ CHICKEN DRUMSTICKS

INGREDIENTS:

- ❖ 8 chicken drumsticks
- ❖ 1/4 cup olive oil
- ❖ 1 teaspoon garlic powder
- ❖ 1 teaspoon onion powder
- ❖ 1 teaspoon smoked paprika
- ❖ 1/2 teaspoon salt
- ❖ 1/2 teaspoon black pepper
- ❖ 1 cup BBQ sauce (store-bought or homemade)
- ❖ Fresh parsley, chopped (for garnish, optional)

INSTRUCTIONS:

1. Get ready with the drumsticks:
2. Dry the chicken drumsticks with paper towels. In a large bowl, mix the drumsticks with black pepper, onion powder, smoked paprika, and olive oil. Make sure that all of the drumsticks are evenly covered.
3. Get the air fryer hot to use.
4. Warm up the air fryer to 190°C (375°F) for five minutes.
5. Get the drumsticks ready:
6. Stack the drumsticks in the air fryer basket so that they are all around the same edge. During the 20 minutes that it's baking at 375°F (190°C), flip the dish over once.
7. While they are still hot, brush the drumsticks with BBQ sauce to make a glaze. Place the drumsticks on a baking

sheet and cover them with more BBQ sauce. For 5 to 10 minutes, or until they are fully cooked and 165°F (74°C) on the inside, the potatoes should be done.

8. Before you serve the drumsticks, take them out of the air fryer and let them cool down. To make it look nicer, you can add chopped parsley on top. Add more BBQ sauce next to the food.

NOTE:

➢ For the final five minutes of cooking, you can raise the temperature to 400°F (204°C) for extra crispy skin.
➢ Dilute the heavier BBQ sauce with water to make applying it to the drumsticks easier.

INGREDIENTS:

❖ Chicken breasts or legs that are 1 pound and have been cut into bite-sized pieces.
❖ 1/4 cup soy sauce
❖ 2 tablespoons honey
❖ 2 tablespoons mirin (or rice vinegar)
❖ 1 tablespoon brown sugar
❖ 1 tablespoon sesame oil
❖ 2 cloves garlic, minced
❖ 1 teaspoon grated ginger
❖ 1/2 teaspoon black pepper
❖ 1 tablespoon cornstarch (optional for thickening the sauce)
❖ 1 tablespoon water (optional for thickening the sauce)
❖ Sesame seeds for garnish (optional)
❖ Sliced green onions for garnish (optional)

INSTRUCTIONS:

1. Get the marinade ready:
2. Mix the brown sugar, sesame oil, honey, mirin, soy sauce, chopped garlic, grated ginger, and black pepper in a medium-sized bowl.
3. Give the chicken a marinade.
4. Coat chicken evenly in marinade. At least 30 minutes is recommended but cover and chill for two hours for optimum taste.
5. Heat the Air Fryer: Set the air fryer's temperature to 380°F (193°C) for five minutes.
6. Prepare the Chicken Bites by removing the chicken pieces from the marinade and allowing any extra to fall off. Place the chicken pieces in a single layer within the air fryer basket. Achieve a temperature of 165°F (74°C) inside the chicken by cooking it at 380°F (193°C) for 12 to 15 minutes and shaking the basket every halfway through.
7. Thicken the Sauce (Optional): Transfer the leftover marinade to a small skillet and heat it while the chicken cooks. Heat to a boil in a medium setting. Make a slurry by combining the cornstarch and water in a small bowl. Stir the slurry into the pot for one to two minutes. Minimize heat.
8. Coat the Chicken: Once the chicken bits are cooked, move them to a big bowl. Toss the chicken evenly in the thickened sauce to coat it evenly.

Serve:

➢ Top the Teriyaki Chicken Bites with sliced green onions and sesame seeds if desired. Serve hot with vegetables or over steaming rice.

NOTE:

➢ Tamari or gluten-free soy sauce makes this recipe gluten-free.
➢ Add a small red pepper flakes to the marinade for a hotter variation.

8. GARLIC PARMESAN CHICKEN WINGS

INGREDIENTS:

- ❖ 2 pounds chicken wings, separated into flats and drumettes
- ❖ 2 tablespoons olive oil
- ❖ 1 teaspoon garlic powder
- ❖ 1 teaspoon onion powder
- ❖ 1 teaspoon smoked paprika
- ❖ 1/2 teaspoon salt
- ❖ 1/4 teaspoon black pepper
- ❖ 1/2 cup grated Parmesan cheese
- ❖ 2 tablespoons butter, melted
- ❖ 2 cloves garlic, minced
- ❖ Chopped fresh parsley for garnish (optional)

INSTRUCTIONS:

1. To prepare the wings, pat them dry using paper towels. Toss the wings in a big bowl with olive oil, salt, black pepper, smoked paprika, onion powder, and garlic powder until well-covered.
2. Heat the Air Fryer: Set the air fryer's temperature to 380°F (193°C) for five minutes.
3. Cook the Wings: Put the wings in a single layer within the air fryer basket. If necessary, cook in batches to prevent crowding. Shake the basket midway through air-frying

the wings for 25–30 minutes at 380°F/193°C until crispy and the inside temperature reaches 165°F (74°C).

4. While the wings cook, prepare the garlic parmesan coating by melting the butter in a small saucepan over medium heat. Cook the minced garlic for one to two minutes or until it becomes aromatic. After taking off the heat, add the grated Parmesan cheese.

5. Coat the Wings: After cooking, transfer the wings to a large dish. Drizzle the wings with the garlic-Parmesan mixture, tossing to coat thoroughly.

Serve:

➢ If preferred, sprinkle some freshly chopped parsley on top of the wings. Warm them up and pair them with your preferred dipping sauce.

NOTE:

➢ For extra crispy wings, you can raise the temperature to 400°F (204°C) for the final five minutes of cooking.
➢ You can change the amount of Parmesan and garlic to suit your tastes.

9. CAJUN SPICED CHICKEN BREASTS

INGREDIENTS:

- ❖ 2 boneless, skinless chicken breasts
- ❖ 1 tablespoon olive oil
- ❖ 1 teaspoon paprika
- ❖ 1 teaspoon garlic powder
- ❖ 1 teaspoon onion powder
- ❖ 1 teaspoon dried thyme
- ❖ 1 teaspoon dried oregano
- ❖ 1/2 teaspoon cayenne pepper (adjust to taste)
- ❖ 1/2 teaspoon salt
- ❖ 1/2 teaspoon black pepper
- ❖ Lemon wedges (for serving)
- ❖ Fresh parsley, chopped (for garnish, optional)

INSTRUCTIONS:

1. Prepare the chicken:
2. Pat chicken breasts dry with paper towels. To cook thick chicken breasts evenly, smash them.
3. This is Cajun Spice Mix. Pepper, onion powder, garlic powder, thyme, and black pepper should all be mixed in a small bowl.
4. Start with seasoning chicken. After using olive oil, cover the breasts evenly with Cajun spices.
5. Heat the Air Fryer: Air fried at 380°F (193°C) for five minutes.

6. Prepare Chicken: Place seasoned chicken breasts in the air fryer basket in a single layer. Turn the chicken halfway through cooking at 380°F/193°C for 12–15 minutes until it reaches 165°F (74°C).
7. Remove air-fried chicken breasts and let them rest before serving. Add finely chopped fresh parsley and lemon slices to squeeze over the top.

NOTE:

➢ The amount of cayenne pepper can be changed to suit your heat tolerance. If it tastes softer, use less or leave it out altogether.
➢ Serve the Cajun-spiced chicken breasts with roasted veggies or a crisp salad for a full supper.

10. HONEY MUSTARD CHICKEN SKEWERS

INGREDIENTS:

- ❖ Chicken breasts or legs that are 1 pound and have been cut into bite-sized pieces.
- ❖ 1/4 cup Dijon mustard
- ❖ 2 tablespoons honey
- ❖ 2 tablespoons olive oil
- ❖ 1 tablespoon apple cider vinegar
- ❖ 2 cloves garlic, minced
- ❖ 1 teaspoon dried thyme
- ❖ 1/2 teaspoon salt
- ❖ 1/4 teaspoon black pepper
- ❖ Wooden or metal skewers
- ❖ Chopped fresh parsley for garnish (optional)

INSTRUCTIONS:

1. To make the marinade, put olive oil, apple cider vinegar, honey, Dijon mustard, chopped garlic, dried thyme, salt, and black pepper in a medium-sized bowl.
2. Toss the chicken in the sauce until it is completely covered. At least 30 minutes is good but cover and chill for two hours for the best taste.
3. Warm up the air fryer: 380°F (193°C) air-fried for five minutes.
4. Get the skewers ready:
5. Evenly thread pieces of chicken that have been marinating onto skewers.

6. When you're ready to cook the skewers, put them in the air fryer basket in a single layer. Once the chicken hits 165°F (74°C), turn it over and cook it for another 10 to 12 minutes at 380°F/193°C.

Take the skewers out of the air fryer and let them cool before serving. Adding fresh parsley is optional. For extra flavor, serve hot with honey mustard sauce.

NOTE:

➢ For 30 minutes, soak the wooden skewers in water before you put the chicken on them. In the
➢ air fryer, this will keep them from getting burned.
➢ Adding bell pepper, onions, or zucchini to the skewers will make them a full meal. You can also change the time it cooks.

11. CRISPY CHICKEN SCHNITZEL

INGREDIENTS:

- ❖ 2 boneless, skinless chicken breasts
- ❖ 1/2 cup all-purpose flour
- ❖ 2 large eggs
- ❖ 1 cup panko breadcrumbs
- ❖ 1/2 cup grated Parmesan cheese
- ❖ 1 teaspoon garlic powder
- ❖ 1 teaspoon onion powder
- ❖ 1/2 teaspoon paprika
- ❖ 1/2 teaspoon salt
- ❖ 1/4 teaspoon black pepper
- ❖ Cooking spray
- ❖ Lemon wedges (for serving)
- ❖ Chopped fresh parsley for garnish (optional)

INSTRUCTIONS:

1. Put the chicken breasts on a piece of paper or plastic wrap. Use a meat tool or rolling pin to pound the chicken until it's 1/4 inch thick.
2. Make Breading Stations: Set up a breading station with three small bowls. Put flour in the first bowl. In another bowl, beat eggs. In the third bowl, add panko breadcrumbs, grated Parmesan, paprika, onion and garlic powders, salt, and black pepper.
3. Bread chicken breasts by coating and shaking off excess flour.

4. Shake excess egg from the floured chicken breast in the beaten egg.
5. Coat the chicken breast with panko breadcrumbs and gently press it down for a uniform coating.
6. Preheat the air fryer for five minutes at 400°F (204°C).
7. To make Schnitzel Chicken
8. , place breaded chicken breasts in a single layer in the air fryer basket. Lightly spray the chicken tops with cooking spray to crisp them.
9. Turn the chicken halfway through cooking it for 10 to 12 minutes at 400°F (204°C) until it is cooked through, golden brown, and 165°F (74°C).

Serve:

➢ Take the chicken schnitzel from the air fryer and rest for a few minutes. Finely chopped fresh parsley and serve with lemon wedges if preferred.

NOTE:

➢ You can double-coat the chicken by doing the egg and breadcrumb stages again for an extra crispy texture.
➢ For a full dinner, serve the chicken schnitzel with zesty coleslaw, fresh salad, or mashed potatoes.

12. RANCH CHICKEN STRIPS

INGREDIENTS:

- ❖ 1 pound chicken breasts cut into strips without any bones or skin
- ❖ 1 cup buttermilk
- ❖ 1 packet ranch seasoning mix
- ❖ 1 cup panko breadcrumbs
- ❖ 1/2 cup grated Parmesan cheese
- ❖ 1/2 teaspoon garlic powder
- ❖ 1/2 teaspoon onion powder
- ❖ 1/2 teaspoon paprika
- ❖ 1/2 teaspoon salt
- ❖ 1/4 teaspoon black pepper
- ❖ Cooking spray
- ❖ Ranch dressing for serving (optional)

INSTRUCTIONS:

1. Marinate the chicken by combining half of the ranch seasoning mix and buttermilk in a large basin. After adding, make sure the chicken strips are thoroughly covered. Cover and chill for up to two hours for maximum flavor, but at least thirty minutes is preferred.
2. To make the breading, combine the panko breadcrumbs, grated Parmesan cheese, paprika, onion, garlic, and black pepper in a shallow bowl. Add the remaining ranch seasoning mix to the breadcrumb mixture.
3. Warm up the air fryer.

4. Preheat the air fryer for five minutes to 400°F (204°C).
5. Bread the Chicken: Shake off excess buttermilk marinade from the chicken strips. After dredging each strip in breadcrumbs, carefully press each strip to coat evenly.
6. Cook Chicken Strips: Place single-layer breaded chicken strips in an air fryer basket. Lightly coat the chicken tops with cooking spray to crisp them.
7. It will take 10 to 12 minutes of cooking at 400°F (204°C) for the chicken strips to reach 165°F (74°C).

Remove air-fried chicken strips and let them rest before serving. Ranch dressing can be served for dipping.

NOTE:

➢ You can double-coat the chicken by doing the breadcrumb and buttermilk stages again for more crispy chicken strips.
➢ For a full supper, serve the ranch chicken strips with vegetable sticks, a fresh salad, and a side of fries.

13. KOREAN BBQ CHICKEN WINGS

INGREDIENTS:

- ❖ 2 pounds chicken wings, separated into flats and drumettes
- ❖ 1 tablespoon olive oil
- ❖ 1/2 teaspoon salt
- ❖ 1/4 teaspoon black pepper
- ❖ For the Korean BBQ Sauce:
- ❖ 1/4 cup soy sauce
- ❖ 2 tablespoons gochujang (Korean chili paste)
- ❖ 2 tablespoons honey
- ❖ 2 tablespoons brown sugar
- ❖ 1 tablespoon rice vinegar
- ❖ 1 tablespoon sesame oil
- ❖ 3 cloves garlic, minced
- ❖ 1 teaspoon grated ginger
- ❖ 1 teaspoon toasted sesame seeds
- ❖ Sliced green onions for garnish (optional)

INSTRUCTIONS:

1. To prepare the wings, pat them dry using paper towels. In a big bowl, combine olive oil, salt, and black pepper. Coat the wings equally.
2. Heat the Air Fryer: Set the air fryer's temperature to 380°F (193°C) for five minutes.
3. The wings should be in a single layer in the air fryer basket. Avoid crowding by cooking in batches. Shake the

basket midway through air-frying the wings for 25–30 minutes at 380°F/193°C until crispy and the inside temperature reaches 165°F (74°C).

4. Prepare Korean BBQ sauce.
5. Make the sauce while the wings cook. Mix soy sauce, gochujang, brown sugar, rice vinegar, sesame oil and minced garlic, grated ginger in a medium bowl.
6. Coat Wings: Transfer cooked wings to a large plate. Cover the wings with Korean BBQ sauce and toss.

➢ If desired, garnish wings with sliced green onions and toasted sesame seeds. Heat food.

NOTE:

➢ On taste, adjust the gochujang amount according on how spicy you like it. Use less gochujang if you'd rather a softer taste.
➢ Before combining the sauce with the wings, simmer it in a small saucepan over medium heat for a few minutes until it thickens slightly for an extra sticky coating.

14. LEMON PEPPER CHICKEN WINGS

INGREDIENTS:

- ❖ 2 pounds chicken wings, separated into flats and drumettes
- ❖ 2 tablespoons olive oil
- ❖ 1 teaspoon salt
- ❖ 1/2 teaspoon black pepper
- ❖ 1 teaspoon baking powder (optional for extra crispiness)

For the Lemon Pepper Sauce:

- ❖ 3 tablespoons unsalted butter, melted
- ❖ 1 tablespoon lemon zest (from about 1-2 lemons)
- ❖ 1 tablespoon lemon juice
- ❖ 1 teaspoon freshly ground black pepper
- ❖ 1/2 teaspoon garlic powder
- ❖ 1/4 teaspoon salt

INSTRUCTIONS:

1. To prepare the wings, pat them dry using paper towels. After being tossed in a big basin with olive oil, salt, black pepper, and baking powder, the wings should be equally coated.
2. Heat the Air Fryer: Set the air fryer's temperature to 380°F (193°C) for five minutes.
3. To prepare the
4. wings, place them in a single layer in the air fryer basket. Cook in batches to avoid crowding. Air-fry the wings for

25–30 minutes at 380°F (193°C) until crispy and 165°F (74°C) inside. Shake the basket halfway through

.

5. Prepare lemon-pepper sauce.
6. Make the sauce while the wings cook. Stir melted butter, lemon zest, lemon juice, freshly ground black pepper, garlic powder, and salt in a small bowl.
7. Coat Wings: Place cooked wings in a big dish. Coat wings in lemon pepper sauce.

Serve

➢ hot chicken wings with lemon zest and freshly ground black pepper, if desired.

NOTE:

➢ Although it's optional, the baking powder makes the wings extremely crispy. You can omit this step if you would rather not utilize it.
➢ Depending on your taste preferences, you can increase the amount of lemon zest or juice in the sauce for a sharper lemon flavor.

15. MEDITERRANEAN CHICKEN KEBABS

INGREDIENTS:

- ❖ Boneless and skinless chicken breasts or thighs sliced into bite-sized chunks
- ❖ 2 tablespoons olive oil
- ❖ 2 tablespoons lemon juice
- ❖ 2 tablespoons plain Greek yogurt
- ❖ 3 cloves garlic, minced
- ❖ 1 tablespoon dried oregano
- ❖ 1 teaspoon ground cumin
- ❖ 1 teaspoon ground coriander
- ❖ 1 teaspoon paprika
- ❖ 1/2 teaspoon salt
- ❖ 1/4 teaspoon black pepper
- ❖ 1 red bell pepper and cut into 1 inch pieces
- ❖ 1 red onion, cut into 1-inch pieces
- ❖ Wooden or metal skewers
- ❖ Fresh parsley, chopped (for garnish, optional)
- ❖ Lemon wedges (for serving)

INSTRUCTIONS:

1. Get the marinade ready.
2. Olive oil, lemon juice, Greek yogurt, minced garlic, dried oregano, ground cumin, coriander, paprika, salt, and black pepper should all be combined in a big bowl.
3. Give the chicken a marinade.

4. Cover chicken pieces evenly with marinade. Cover and chill for two hours for optimal flavor, but thirty minutes is prefer
5. able.Make skewers:
6. Skewer-marinated chicken, red onion, and bell pepper.
7. Hot Air Fryer: 380°F air-fried for 5 minutes.
8. Place one layer of chicken kebabs in the air fryer basket. Cook chicken at 380°F (193°C) for 12–15 minutes, rotating halfway, until 165°F (74°C).

After air-frying, let the kebabs settle before serving. Squeeze lemon slices and sprinkle fresh parsley.

NOTE:

➢ To avoid the chicken and veggies in the air fryer burning, soak wooden skewers in water for at least half an hour before threading them.
➢ Try these kebabs with fresh Greek salad, hummus, or a side of tzatziki sauce for a whole Mediterranean supper.

16. SRIRACHA HONEY CHICKEN THIGHS

INGREDIENTS:

- ❖ 1 pound boneless, skinless chicken thighs
- ❖ 2 tablespoons olive oil
- ❖ 1/4 cup honey
- ❖ 2 tablespoons Sriracha sauce (adjust to taste)
- ❖ 2 tablespoons soy sauce
- ❖ 1 tablespoon rice vinegar
- ❖ 2 cloves garlic, minced
- ❖ 1/2 teaspoon ground ginger
- ❖ 1/4 teaspoon salt
- ❖ 1/4 teaspoon black pepper
- ❖ Chopped green onions for garnish (optional)
- ❖ Sesame seeds for garnish (optional)

INSTRUCTIONS:

1. Get the marinade ready.
2. Mix rice vinegar, honey, ground ginger, garlic, Sriracha sauce, soy sauce, salt, and black pepper in a small bowl.
3. To marinate the chicken, put the thighs in a big dish or a plastic bag that can be sealed. Pour the marinade over each piece of chicken to ensure it is thoroughly coated. Let it marinate in the fridge for at least half an hour or, for maximum flavor, up to two hours.
4. Heat the Air Fryer: Set the air fryer's temperature to 380°F (193°C) for five minutes.

5. Cook the Chicken Thighs: Take the thighs out of the marinade and let any extra fall off. Place the chicken thighs in a single layer within the air fryer basket.
6. Turn he chicken halfway through cooking at 380°F (193°C) for 15–18 minutes until it reaches 165°F (74°C). chicken skin should be well-browned.

Remove air-fried chicken thighs and let them rest before serving. If desired, add green onions and sesame seeds. Serve with favorite sides after heating.

*Add sesame seeds and green onions if preferred. Heat and serve with preferred side*s.

NOTE:

➢ Pat the chicken thighs dry before marinating, then gently sprinkle them with flour or cornstarch before cooking for extra crispy chicken.
➢ Adjust the amount of Sriracha to make it as spicy as you like. Reduce the amount of Sriracha if you prefer it softer.

INGREDIENT:

- ❖ Bites of 1 pound boneless, skinless chicken breasts or thighs
- ❖ 1/2 cup all-purpose flour
- ❖ 1/2 cup cornstarch
- ❖ 2 large eggs, beaten
- ❖ 1 cup panko breadcrumbs
- ❖ 1/2 cup grated Parmesan cheese
- ❖ 1/2 teaspoon garlic powder
- ❖ 1/2 teaspoon onion powder
- ❖ 1/2 teaspoon salt
- ❖ 1/4 teaspoon black pepper
- ❖ Cooking spray

For the Sweet and Sour Sauce:

- ❖ 1/2 cup ketchup
- ❖ 1/4 cup rice vinegar
- ❖ 1/4 cup honey
- ❖ 2 tablespoons soy sauce
- ❖ 2 tablespoons water, 1 tablespoon cornstarch
- ❖ 1/2 teaspoon minced garlic
- ❖ 1/2 teaspoon minced ginger

INSTRUCTIONS:

1. Chicken Bites are made by mixing flour and cornstarch in a shallow bowl. Beat eggs in another bowl. In a third bowl, combine panko breadcrumbs, grated Parmesan, onion and garlic powders, salt, and black pepper.
2. Bread the Chicken: Shake off excess flour after dredging each chicken piece.
3. Dip the floured chicken piece into the beaten egg mixture to shake off excess egg.
4. Coat the chicken piece with breadcrumbs and gently press it down for a uniform coating.
5. Heat the Air Fryer: Air fry at 380°F (193°C) for five minutes.
6. In the air fryer basket, place the breaded chicken bites in a single layer. Lightly spray cooking spray on top to crisp.
7. Cook the chicken bites for 12–15 minutes at 380°F (193°C), shaking the basket halfway through, until they reach 165°F (74°C).
8. Make the sour and
9. sweet sauce by combining ketchup, rice vinegar, honey, soy sauce, minced ginger, and garlic in a saucepan. Simmer on medium heat.
10. Mix cornstarch and water for a slurry. The sauce will thicken after stirring the slurry into the pot for one to two minutes. Get off the heat.
11. Coat the Chicken: Transfer cooked chicken parts to a large bowl. Coat the chicken evenly in sweet and sour sauce.

Serve:

> ➢ Warm the tangy and sweet chicken pieces. If desired, add sesame seeds or chopped green onions.

NOTE:

> ➢ You can double-coat the chicken by following the breadcrumb and egg recipes for even more crunch.
> ➢ Add a little red pepper flakes to the sweet and sour sauce for a hotter variation.

18. PESTO CHICKEN BREASTS

INGREDIENTS:

- ➢ 2 boneless, skinless chicken breasts
- ➢ 1/4 cup pesto (store-bought or homemade)
- ➢ 1 tablespoon olive oil
- ➢ 1/4 teaspoon salt
- ➢ 1/4 teaspoon black pepper
- ➢ 1/4 cup grated Parmesan cheese (optional)
- ➢ Fresh basil leaves for garnish (optional)

INSTRUCTIONS:

1. Prepare chicken.
2. Pat chicken breasts dry with paper towels. If thick, pound them to an equal thickness before cooking.
3. Chicken Seasoning:
4. Rub olive oil, salt, and black pepper on chicken breasts.
5. Apply pesto:
6. Apply pesto evenly to each chicken breast. Grated Parmesan cheese adds flavor.
7. Prepare the air fryer.
8. Pre-heat the air fryer for 5 minutes at 380°F (193°C).
9. Cook chicken:
10. Place chicken breasts in air fryer basket in a single layer. Turn the chicken halfway through cooking at 380°F (193°C) for 15–18 minutes until it reaches 165°F (74°C).

Serve:

> ➤ Remove chicken breasts from air fryer and let rest for a few minutes. Add fresh basil if desired. Serve hot with roasted veggies or a fresh salad.

NOTE:

> ➤ For a twist, you can add sliced cherry tomatoes or thinly sliced red onions to the pesto before air-frying.
> ➤ You can also use different types of pesto, such as sun-dried tomato pesto or basil walnut pesto, for varying flavors.

19. SAME GINGER, CHICKEN WINGS

INGREDIENTS:

- ❖ 2 pounds chicken wings, separated into flats and drumettes
- ❖ 1 tablespoon olive oil
- ❖ 1/4 teaspoon salt
- ❖ 1/4 teaspoon black pepper

For the sesame-ginger Ginger Sauce:

- ❖ 1/4 cup soy sauce
- ❖ 2 tablespoons honey
- ❖ 2 tablespoons sesame oil
- ❖ 1 tablespoon rice vinegar
- ❖ 2 tablespoons grated fresh ginger
- ❖ 2 cloves garlic, minced
- ❖ 1 tablespoon sesame seeds
- ❖ Heat-optional 1/4 tsp red pepper flakes
- ❖ Sliced green onions for garnish (optional)
- ❖ Extra sesame seeds for garnish (optional)

INSTRUCTIONS:

1. Dry wings with paper towels. Mix olive oil, salt, and black pepper in a big bowl. Coat wings equally.
2. Air Fryer: Heat to 380°F (193°C) for 5 minutes.

3. Place wings in air fryer basket in single layer. Cook in batches to reduce crowding. Air-fry wings at 380°F (193°C) for 25–30 minutes, shaking the basket halfway through, until crispy and 165°F (74°C).
4. To make Sesame Ginger Sauce: Prepare sauce while wings fry. Use a small skillet to mix soy sauce, honey, sesame oil, rice vinegar, minced garlic, ginger, and red pepper flakes. Simmer, stirring, over medium heat for 3–4 minutes to thicken the sauce. Stir in sesame seeds.
5. Transfer cooked wings to a large dish to coat. Toss wings in sesame ginger sauce to coat
   ➤ .If desired, serve wings with more sesame seeds and green onions.

NOTE:

➤ For added crunch, sprinkle toasted sesame seeds on top before serving.
➤ Taste and adjust red pepper flakes for spiciness.

20. CHIPOTLE LIME CHICKEN TENDERS

INGREDIENT:

- ❖ Boneless, skinless chicken breast strips—1 pound
- ❖ 1 tablespoon olive oil
- ❖ 1 tablespoon lime juice (freshly squeezed)
- ❖ 1 tablespoon chipotle chili powder
- ❖ 1 teaspoon smoked paprika
- ❖ 1 teaspoon garlic powder
- ❖ 1/2 teaspoon onion powder
- ❖ 1/2 teaspoon ground cumin
- ❖ 1/2 teaspoon salt
- ❖ 1/4 teaspoon black pepper
- ❖ Cooking spray

INSTRUCTIONS:

1. Get the marinade ready.
2. Mix olive oil, lime juice, smoked paprika, chipotle chili powder, onion powder, ground cumin, salt, and black pepper in a large bowl.
3. Give the chicken a marinade.
4. Toss the chicken tenders in the marinade-coated basin to ensure a consistent coating. For a stronger flavor, cover and chill for up to two hours, but at least thirty minutes is preferred.
5. Warm up the air fryer.
6. Preheat the air fryer for five minutes to 380°F (193°C).
7. Cook the tenders of chicken:

8. Place the marinated chicken tenders in the air fryer basket in a single layer. Lightly spray cooking spray over the tops to help them crisp up.

9. Turn the chicken tenders halfway through cooking at 380°F (193°C) for 10–12 minutes until they reach 165°F (74°C).

To serve, remove the chicken tenders from the air fryer and let them settle. Accompany the dish with extra lime wedges for squeezing and your preferred dipping sauce.

NOTE:

➢ To adjust for heat, adjust the amount of chipotle chili powder. Reduce or leave out the chipotle powder if you have a softer taste.

➢ To give the chicken tenders more freshness, you can add some chopped cilantro as a garnish before serving.

21. CLASSIC FRENCH FRIES

INGREDIENTS:

- ❖ 4 large russet potatoes
- ❖ 2 tablespoons olive oil
- ❖ 1 teaspoon salt
- ❖ 1/2 teaspoon black pepper
- ❖ 1/2 teaspoon paprika (optional for extra flavor)

INSTRUCTIONS:

1. If preferred, cut the potatoes into thin strips about 1/4 inch thick after peeling them. Try to maintain the fries' uniform size throughout frying.
2. To soak the potatoes, put them in a big dish of cold water with the potato strips. Soak for up to two hours, but at least thirty minutes. This makes fries crispier by assisting in the removal of extra starch.
3. After draining, pat potatoes dry with a clean kitchen towel or paper towel. Making fries dry helps them crisp.
4. Coat the potato strips evenly with olive oil, salt, black pepper, and paprika (if using) in a large bowl.
5. Heat the Air Fryer: Air fried at 380°F (193°C) for five minutes.
6. Cook the Fries: Put the potato strips in the air fryer basket in a single layer. If necessary, cook in batches to prevent crowding. Fries should be air-fried for 15 to 20 minutes at 380°F (193°C), shaking the basket halfway

through, or until they are crispy and golden brown. The precise cooking time may change depending on your air fryer type and the fries' thickness.

Remove fries from oven and cool before serving. Serve with your favorite dipping sauces after warming.

NOTE:

➢ Halfway through the cooking time, you can spray the fries with cooking spray for even more crunch.
➢ Alter the cooking time if you prefer thicker fries to ensure they are crispy and thoroughly cooked.

22. SWEET POTATO FRIES

INGREDIENTS:

- ❖ 2 large sweet potatoes
- ❖ 2 tablespoons olive oil
- ❖ 1 teaspoon salt
- ❖ 1/2 teaspoon black pepper
- ❖ 1/2 teaspoon paprika
- ❖ 1/2 teaspoon garlic powder
- ❖ 1/2 teaspoon ground cumin (optional for extra flavor)
- ❖ 1/4 teaspoon cayenne pepper (optional for heat)

INSTRUCTIONS:

1. After peeling the sweet potatoes, cut them into thin strips about 1/4 inch thick. Try to maintain the fries' uniform size throughout frying.
2. Put the sweet potatoes in a big dish of cold water with the strips to soak them. Soak for up to two hours, but at least thirty minutes. This helps remove starch, making fries crispier.
3. Drain and pat sweet potatoes dry with a clean kitchen towel or paper towel. Drying fries crisps them.
4. Season sweet potatoes with olive oil, salt, black pepper, paprika, garlic powder, ground cumin (if needed), and cayenne pepper in a big bowl. Coat sweet potato strips equally.
5. Heat the Air Fryer: Air fried at 380°F (193°C) for five minutes.
6. Place sweet potato fries in air fryer basket in single layer. Avoid crowding by cooking in batches. The fries should be

air-fried for 15–20 minutes at 380°F (193°C), shaking the basket halfway through, until crispy and golden brown. Air fryer model and fry thickness affect cooking time.

To serve, remove the fries from the air fryer and allow them to cool a little. Warm them up and pair them with your preferred dipping sauces.

NOTE:

- ➢ Halfway through the cooking time, you can give the fries a little coat of cooking spray for even more crunch.
- ➢ Taste and adjust the seasoning. For a sweet variation, you could add a sprinkling of cinnamon or a bit of brown sugar.

23. GARLIC PARMESAN FRIES

INGREDIENTS:

- ❖ 4 large russet potatoes
- ❖ 2 tablespoons olive oil
- ❖ 1 teaspoon salt
- ❖ 1/2 teaspoon black pepper
- ❖ 1/2 teaspoon garlic powder
- ❖ 1/2 teaspoon dried oregano (optional)
- ❖ 1/4 cup grated Parmesan
- ❖ 2-tbsp chopped fresh parsley (as garnish)

INSTRUCTIONS:

1. Cut the potatoes into thin strips that are about 1/4 inch thick after peeling them, if preferred. Try to maintain the fries' uniform size throughout frying.
2. To soak the potatoes, put them in a big dish of cold water with the potato strips. Soak for up to two hours, but at least thirty minutes. This makes fries crispier by assisting in the removal of extra starch.
3. After draining, pat potatoes dry with a clean kitchen towel or paper towel. Making fries dry helps them crisp.
4. Stir the potato strips in olive oil, salt, black pepper, garlic powder, and dried oregano (if using) in a large bowl until evenly coated.
5. Heat the Air Fryer: Heat air fryer to 380°F (193°C) for 5 minutes.
6. Air fried the fries: Place the potato strips in a single layer in the basket. Avoid crowding by cooking in batches. Air-fry fries for 15–20 minutes at 380°F (193°C), shaking the

basket halfway through, until crispy and golden brown. Air fryer type and fry thickness
7. affect cooking time.

Serve:

> ➢ If preferred, garnish with freshly chopped parsley. Warm-up and pair with your preferred dipping sauces.

NOTE:

> ➢ Just before serving, you can add some finely chopped fresh garlic or olive oil infused with garlic to the fries for an additional burst of flavor.
> ➢ Depending on your flavor preferences, adjust the amount of garlic powder and Parmesan cheese.

24. CAJUN SWEET POTATO WEDGES

INGREDIENTS:

- ❖ 2 large sweet potatoes
- ❖ 2 tablespoons olive oil
- ❖ 1 tablespoon Cajun seasoning (store-bought or homemade)
- ❖ 1/2 teaspoon smoked paprika
- ❖ 1/2 teaspoon garlic powder
- ❖ 1/2 teaspoon onion powder
- ❖ 1/4 teaspoon salt
- ❖ 1/4 teaspoon black pepper
- ❖ Chopped fresh parsley for garnish (optional)

INSTRUCTIONS:

1. To prepare the sweet potatoes, peel them if you choose, then cut them into wedges. For consistent frying, try to get wedges of a uniform size.
2. First, coat the sweet potato wedges evenly with olive oil in a big bowl before seasoning.
3. Add the Cajun spice: Sprinkle the sweet potato wedges with the Cajun spice, smoked paprika, garlic powder, onion powder, salt, and black pepper. Toss to make sure the seasoning mixture coats the wedges thoroughly.
4. Heat the Air Fryer: Set the air fryer's temperature for five minutes to 380°F (193°C).
5. Cook the Sweet Potato Wedges: Spread out the seasoned wedges in a single layer into the air fryer basket. If necessary, cook in batches to prevent crowding. The wedges should be air-fried for 15 to 20 minutes at 380°F

(193°C), shaking the basket halfway through or until the outsides are crispy and soft. Depending on the brand of your air fryer and the size of the wedges, the precise cooking time may change.

To serve, take the wedges out of the air fryer and give them a little time to cool. If desired, garnish with freshly chopped parsley. Serve hot as a side dish or with your preferred dipping sauces.

NOTE:

- ➤ A sprinkle of cayenne pepper adds spice.
- ➤ Use a milder seasoning combination or cut back on the Cajun seasoning if you'd rather it taste less strong.

INGREDIENTS:

- ❖ 4 large russet potatoes
- ❖ 2 tablespoons olive oil
- ❖ 1 teaspoon salt
- ❖ 1/2 teaspoon black pepper
- ❖ 1/2 teaspoon garlic powder
- ❖ 1/2 teaspoon paprika
- ❖ 1 cup shredded cheddar cheese
- ❖ 1/2 cup crumbled cooked bacon (about 4 strips)
- ❖ 1/4 cup sliced green onions
- ❖ 1/4 cup sour cream (for drizzling or dipping)
- ❖ Optional: chopped fresh parsley for garnish

INSTRUCTIONS:

1. If desired, peel and cut potatoes into 1/4-inch strips. Frying fries should be consistent in size.
2. Mix potato strips, olive oil, salt, black pepper, garlic powder, and paprika in a big basin.
3. Heat Air Fryer: Heat for 5 minutes at 380°F (193°C).
4. Fried fries. Put potato strips in air fryer basket in single layer. Batch cook to avoid crowding. Air-fry fries at 380°F (193°C) for 15–20 minutes until crispy and golden brown, shaking the basket halfway.
5. Add toppings: Place fries on an oven-safe platter after cooking. Sprinkle cheddar cheese shreds on fries evenly.
6. Return the dish to the air fryer and cook at 350°F (175°C) for three to five minutes until the cheese melts.

7. Remove air-fried loaded cheese fries and serve. Scatter green onions and bacon on top. If preferred, add finely chopped fresh parsley and sour cream.

Serve Hot:

➤ While the fries are still hot and the cheese is still oozy, serve it right away. Savor it with extra sour cream or your preferred dipping sauce.

NOTE:

➤ Before serving, you can optionally top the cheese with a little spicy sauce or smoky paprika for added flavor.
➤ Consider adding extra toppings like caramelized onions or sautéed mushrooms to make the dish more heartier.

INGREDIENTS:

- ❖ Four large russet potatoes
- ❖ 2 tablespoons truffle oil (white or black truffle oil)
- ❖ 1 tablespoon olive oil
- ❖ 1 teaspoon salt
- ❖ 1/2 teaspoon black pepper
- ❖ 1/2 teaspoon garlic powder
- ❖ Dried thyme or rosemary, 1/2 tsp
- ❖ 1/4 cup Parmesan
- ❖ 1 tbsp chopped fresh parsley (optional garnish)
- ❖ Optional truffle oil sprinkle

INSTRUCTIONS:

1. Cut the potatoes into thin strips that are about 1/4 inch thick after peeling them, if preferred. Try to maintain the fries' uniform size throughout frying.
2. To season the potatoes, combine the olive oil, truffle oil, salt, black pepper, garlic powder, and dried thyme or rosemary (if using) in a big basin and toss until the potato strips are equally coated.
3. Heat the Air Fryer: Set the air fryer's temperature for five minutes to 380°F (193°C).
4. Cook the Fries: Place potato strips in air fryer basket in a single layer.If necessary, cook in batches to prevent crowding. Fries should be air-fried for 15 to 20 minutes at 380°F (193°C), shaking the basket halfway through, or until they are crispy and golden brown.

5. Add the Parmesan cheese: As soon as the fries are done, move them to a big bowl. Grate some Parmesan cheese over the fries while they're still hot, then toss to coat evenly.

To serve, sprinkle some finely chopped fresh parsley on top and, if you like, drizzle with a little more truffle oil. Warm up the food.

NOTE:

➢ The flavor of truffle oil is strong, so use it sparingly. Make adjustments based on your personal preferences.

➢ Serve these fries with a truffle aioli or dipping sauce for an extra treat.

INGREDIENTS:

- ❖ 4 large russet potatoes
- ❖ 2 tablespoons olive oil
- ❖ 1 teaspoon salt
- ❖ 1/2 teaspoon black pepper
- ❖ 1/2 teaspoon paprika
- ❖ 1/2 teaspoon garlic powder
- ❖ 1/2 teaspoon onion powder
- ❖ 1/2 teaspoon cayenne pepper (optional for heat)
- ❖ 1 teaspoon dried thyme or oregano (optional for extra flavor)

INSTRUCTIONS:

1. Peel the potatoes if you'd like to prepare them. Spiralize or use a curly fry cutter to chop the potatoes into curly forms. You can cut them into ordinary fries or use a regular spiralizer if you don't have a curly fry cutter.
2. Toss the curly fries in a big dish of olive oil until they are equally covered. This is how you season the potatoes. Add salt, black pepper, paprika, cayenne pepper (if used), dried thyme or oregano, garlic, and onion powder. Stir in seasoning.
3. Heat Air Fryer: Heat for 5 minutes at 380°F (193°C).
4. Single-layer curly fries in air fryer basket. Cooking them in batches might be necessary to prevent crowding. Fries should be air-fried for 15 to 20 minutes at 380°F (193°C), shaking the basket halfway through or until they are crispy and golden brown. Depending on your air fryer

type and the fries' thickness, the precise cooking time may change.

5. Serving suggestions: Take the curly fries out of the air fryer and let them cool a little. Warm-up and pair with your preferred dipping sauces.

NOTE:

➢ Halfway through the cooking time, you can give the fries a little coat of cooking spray for even more crunch.

➢ Change the amount of cayenne pepper or add a little sprinkle of chili powder if you like your food hotter.

INGREDIENTS:

- ❖ 3 medium zucchini
- ❖ 1/2 cup all-purpose flour
- ❖ 2 large eggs, beaten
- ❖ 1 cup panko breadcrumbs
- ❖ 1/4 cup grated Parmesan cheese
- ❖ 1/2 teaspoon garlic powder
- ❖ 1/2 teaspoon onion powder
- ❖ 1/2 teaspoon dried oregano or basil (optional)
- ❖ 1/4 teaspoon salt
- ❖ 1/4 teaspoon black pepper
- ❖ Cooking spray

INSTRUCTIONS:

1. Prepare zucchini by washing and drying. Slice them into 1/4-1/2-inch fries or sticks.
2. Create a Breading Station:
3. Place three small dishes at a breading station. Place flour in the first bowl. Transfer beaten eggs to second bowl. In the third bowl, mix panko breadcrumbs, grated Parmesan cheese, dried oregano or basil (if preferred), onion powder, garlic powder, and black pepper.
4. Roll Zucchini:
5. Flour each zucchini stick and shake off excess. Lean and drop into beaten eggs. Cover with breadcrumbs and press gently to stick.
6. Heat the Air Fryer: Heat air fryer to 380°F (193°C) for 5 minutes.

7. Cook Zucchini Fries: Place breaded zucchini fries in air fryer basket in a single layer. Lightly spray top with cooking spray to crisp. Shake the basket halfway through cooking fries for 10–12 minutes at 380°F/193°C until crispy and golden brown. Air fryer type and zucchini thickness determine cooking time.

Serve zucchini fries after cooling from the air fryer. Serve hot with ranch, marinara, or garlic aioli.

NOTE:

➢ Double-coat zucchini fries by repeating breadcrumb and egg steps for more crunch.
➢ For added spice, add a sprinkle of red pepper flakes to the breadcrumbs.

29. SEASONED POTATO WEDGES

INGREDIENTS:

- ❖ 4 large russet potatoes
- ❖ 2 tablespoons olive oil
- ❖ 1 teaspoon salt
- ❖ 1/2 teaspoon black pepper
- ❖ 1/2 teaspoon paprika
- ❖ 1/2 teaspoon garlic powder
- ❖ 1/2 teaspoon onion powder
- ❖ 1/2 teaspoon dried rosemary/thyme (optional)
- ❖ 1/4 teaspoon cayenne pepper (optional for heat)

INSTRUCTIONS:

1. Wash and scrape the potatoes to prepare them. Chop them into wedges that are half an inch thick. Try to maintain as much consistency in the size of the wedges for more even cooking.
2. Toss the potato wedges in a big bowl of olive oil until they are equally covered. This is how you season the potatoes. Add onion powder, garlic powder, paprika, salt, black pepper, dried thyme or rosemary, and cayenne pepper. Toss well to distribute spice evenly.
3. Heat the Air Fryer: Set the air fryer's temperature for five minutes to 380°F (193°C).
4. Cook the Potato Wedges: Put the seasoned potato wedges in a single layer within the air fryer basket. If necessary, cook in batches to prevent crowding. Shake the basket halfway through the air fry period and cook the wedges for 15 to 20 minutes at 380°F/193°C, or until they are

crispy and golden brown. Depending on the model of your air fryer and the thickness of the wedges, the precise cooking time may change.

To serve, take the potato wedges out of the air fryer and give them a little time to cool. Serve hot as a side dish or with your preferred dipping sauces.

NOTE:

➢ Halfway through cooking, give the wedges a small mist of cooking spray for even more crunch.
➢ Feel free to add extra spices for a different twist, or to modify the seasoning to your personal taste, such as chile powder or Parmesan cheese.

30. ROSEMARY GARLIC FRIES

INGREDIENTS:

- ❖ Four large russet potatoes
- ❖ 2 tablespoons olive oil
- ❖ 1 teaspoon salt
- ❖ 1/2 teaspoon black pepper
- ❖ 1 teaspoon garlic powder
- ❖ tsp dried rosemary (or finely chopped fresh rosemary)
- ❖ 1/2 teaspoon onion powder
- ❖ 1/4 teaspoon paprika (optional for extra color)
- ❖ 1-2 cloves garlic, minced (optional for extra garlic flavor)

INSTRUCTIONS:

1. Wash and scrape potatoes to prepare. Cut them into 1/4–1/2-inch wedges or strips.
2. Toss the potato strips in olive oil in a big bowl until they are equally covered. This is how you season the potatoes. Add the onion powder, paprika (if using), dried or fresh rosemary, garlic powder, salt, and black pepper. To guarantee that the spice is dispersed equally, toss thoroughly.
3. Heat the Air Fryer: Set the air fryer's temperature for five minutes to 380°F (193°C).
4. Cook the Fries: Spread out the seasoned potato strips in a single layer into the air fryer basket. If necessary, cook in batches to prevent crowding. Fries should be air-fried for 15 to 20 minutes at 380°F (193°C), shaking the basket halfway through, or until they are crispy and golden

brown. To avoid burning, add minced garlic to the basket in the last five minutes.

To serve, take the fries out of the air fryer and allow them to cool a little. Warm up and pair with your preferred dipping sauces.

NOTE:

➢ Halfway through the frying time, lightly mist the fries with cooking spray for even more crunch.
➢ Use fresh rosemary if available, as it imparts a stronger taste. Crush the dried rosemary slightly if using it to get additional taste.
➢ You can increase the amount of minced garlic in the seasoning mixture if you want your fries quite garlicky.

INGREDIENTS:

- ❖ 4 large russet potatoes
- ❖ 2 tablespoons olive oil
- ❖ 1 teaspoon salt
- ❖ 1/2 teaspoon black pepper
- ❖ 1 teaspoon chili powder
- ❖ 1/2 teaspoon smoked paprika
- ❖ 1/2 teaspoon garlic powder
- ❖ 1/2 teaspoon onion powder
- ❖ 1/4 teaspoon cayenne pepper (adjust to taste for spiciness)
- ❖ optional
- ❖ garnish: 2 tablespoons chopped fresh cilantro
- ❖ Optional s
- ❖ our cream or ranch dressing

INSTRUCTION:

1. Wash and scrape potatoes to prepare. Cut them into 1/4–1/2-inch wedges or strips.
2. Toss the potato strips in olive oil in a big bowl until they are equally covered. This is how you season the potatoes. Add the onion, garlic, and cayenne powders, chile, black pepper, and smoked paprika. To guarantee that the spice is dispersed equally, toss thoroughly.
3. Heat the Air Fryer: Set the air fryer's temperature for five minutes to 380°F (193°C).
4. Cook the Fries: Spread out the seasoned potato strips in a single layer into the air fryer basket. If necessary, cook in

batches to prevent crowding. Fries should be air-fried for 15 to 20 minutes at 380°F (193°C), shaking the basket halfway through, or until they are crispy and golden brown.

5. Optional: Top the fries with shredded cheddar cheese in the final two to three minutes of cooking if you're going to add cheese. Keep heating until the cheese is bubbling and melted.

To serve, take the fries out of the air fryer and allow them to cool a little. If desired, garnish with freshly cut cilantro. Serve hot with ranch or sour cream for dipping.

NOTE:

➢ The amount of cayenne pepper depends on your heat preference.
➢ After frying, you can add extra chili powder or a dash of spicy sauce to the fries for more flavor.

INGREDIENTS:

- ❖ 2 ripe avocados
- ❖ 1/2 cup all-purpose flour
- ❖ 2 large eggs, beaten
- ❖ 1 cup panko breadcrumbs
- ❖ 1/4 cup grated Parmesan cheese
- ❖ 1/2 teaspoon garlic powder
- ❖ 1/2 teaspoon onion powder
- ❖ 1/2 teaspoon paprika
- ❖ 1/4 teaspoon salt
- ❖ 1/4 teaspoon black pepper
- ❖ Cooking spray

INSTRUCTIONS:

1. Cut the avocados in half and remove the pit to prepare the avocados. Remove the meat and slice it into fries or wedges that are about 1/2 inch thick.
2. Establish a Breading Station:
3. Put up three small bowls at a breading station. Put the flour in the first bowl. Transfer the beaten eggs to the second bowl. Combine the panko breadcrumbs, grated Parmesan cheese, paprika, onion, and garlic powders with the salt and black pepper in the third bowl.
4. Spread the Avocado Chips:
5. After shaking off any excess flour, coat each avocado wedge. Lean it over and drop it into the beaten eggs. Next, cover it with the breadcrumb mixture and gently press it to cling.

6. The air fryer should be preheated for five minutes to 375°F (190°C).
7. Cook the Avocado Fries: Put the breaded avocado wedges in a single layer within the air fryer basket. To help them crisp up, lightly spray cooking spray over the tops. Fries should be cooked for 8 to 10 minutes at 375°F (190°C), rotating them halfway through or until they are crispy and golden brown.

Serve: Take the avocado fries out of the air fryer and give them a little time to cool. Serve hot with your preferred dipping sauces, including spicy Sriracha aioli or tart ranch.

NOTE:

- ➤ Since avocado fries soften over time, it's better to eat them fresh. Make sure to use firm but ripe avocados, as overripe ones may become mushy.
- ➤ Add your favorite spices or cayenne pepper to the breadcrumb mixture for taste.

INGREDIENTS:

- ❖ 4 large russet potatoes
- ❖ 2 tablespoons olive oil
- ❖ 1 teaspoon salt
- ❖ 1/2 teaspoon black pepper
- ❖ 1 teaspoon dried oregano
- ❖ 1/2 teaspoon garlic powder
- ❖ 1/2 teaspoon onion powder
- ❖ 1/4 teaspoon paprika
- ❖ 1/4 cup crumbled feta cheese
- ❖ 2 tablespoons chopped fresh parsley
- ❖ 1 tablespoon lemon juice (optional, for extra zest)
- ❖ Tzatziki sauce (optional for serving)

INSTRUCTIONS:

1. Get the potatoes ready:
2. Scrub and wash potatoes. Cut them into 1/4–1/2-inch wedges or strips.
3. Add seasoning to the potatoes:
4. Toss the potato strips in olive oil in a big bowl until they are well coated. Add the paprika, dried oregano, garlic powder, onion powder, black pepper, and salt. To guarantee that the spice is dispersed equally, toss thoroughly.
5. Heat the Air Fryer: Set the air fryer's temperature for five minutes to 380°F (193°C).
6. Cook the Fries: Spread out the seasoned potato strips in a single layer into the air fryer basket. If necessary, cook in

batches to prevent crowding. Fries should be air-fried for 15 to 20 minutes at 380°F (193°C), shaking the basket halfway through, or until they are crispy and golden brown.

7. Add Greek Toppings: As soon as the fries are heated through, scatter the feta cheese crumbles on top. Pour in some lemon juice, if using, and toss to mix.

Serve:

➢ Sprinkle with freshly cut parsley. Serve hot, with tzatziki sauce available for dipping on the side.

NOTE:

➢ Add a few thinly sliced kalamata olives or a pinch of extra-dried oregano for an even stronger Greek taste.

➢ The Greek-style fries go very well with tzatziki sauce, which can be prepared in advance or purchased from the shop. For a fresh dip, if you're creating your own, mix Greek yogurt with grated cucumber, minced garlic, lemon juice, and dill.

INGREDIENTS:

- ❖ 1 cup polenta (cornmeal)
- ❖ 4 cups vegetable or chicken broth
- ❖ 1/4 cup grated Parmesan cheese
- ❖ One tablespoon olive oil
- ❖ 1/2 teaspoon garlic powder
- ❖ 1/2 teaspoon dried oregano or thyme
- ❖ 1/4 teaspoon salt
- ❖ 1/4 teaspoon black pepper
- ❖ Cooking spray

INSTRUCTIONS:

1. To make the polenta, boil the chicken or vegetable stock in a big pot. Lower the heat and mix in the polenta gradually. Stir often for 5–7 minutes until the polenta thickens and peels away from the pot.
2. Cheese and Seasonings: Stir in the olive oil, salt, black pepper, dried oregano or thyme, garlic powder, and grated Parmesan cheese. Blend thoroughly until the cheese melts and the spices are dispersed equally.
3. Assemble the Polenta.
4. Spoon the polenta onto a baking tray or dish lined with paper. Evenly spread it into a layer that is about 1/2 inch thick. Let it cool and set for a minimum of one hour or until it becomes firm. You can put it in the fridge to set it up more quickly.

5. Slice the Polenta into Fries: After the polenta has firmed and set, slice it into sticks the size of fries, about 1/2 inch across.
6. The air fryer should be preheated for five minutes to 400°F (200°C).
7.
8. Cook Polenta Fries: Place fries in the air fryer basket in a single layer. Lightly spray them with cooking spray to crisp up. Cook fries for 10–15 minutes at 400°F (200°C), flipping halfway, until crispy and golden brown.

Remove the air-fried polenta fries and cool before serving. Serve hot with hot ketchup, marinara, or aioli.

NOTE:

> ➢ To enhance flavor, try adding herbs or spices like Italian seasoning or smokey paprika to the
> ➢ polenta mixture.
> ➢ If the polenta fries are soft or cling together, freeze and harden them before slicing and air-frying.

35. PARMESAN HERB SWEET POTATO FRIES

INGREDIENTS:

- ❖ 4 large sweet potatoes
- ❖ 2 tablespoons olive oil
- ❖ 1/2 teaspoon saltw
- ❖ 1/2 teaspoon black pepper
- ❖ 1 teaspoon garlic powder
- ❖ 1 teaspoon dried rosemary or thyme (or a mix of both)
- ❖ 1/2 teaspoon paprika
- ❖ 1/4 cup grated Parmesan cheese
- ❖ 1-2 tablespoons chopped fresh parsley (optional, for garnish)
- ❖ Cooking spray

INSTRUCTIONS:

1. Cut the sweet potatoes into thin fries that are about 1/4 and 1/2 inch thick after peeling them. Try to maintain uniformity in the size of the fries for even frying.
2. Toss the sweet potato fries in a big bowl of olive oil until they are well coated. This is how you season the sweet potatoes. Add the paprika, dried rosemary or thyme, garlic powder, salt, and black pepper. To guarantee that the spice is dispersed equally, toss thoroughly.
3. Heat the Air Fryer: Set the air fryer's temperature for five minutes to 380°F (193°C).
4. Cook the Sweet Potato Fries: Spread out the seasoned fries in a single layer within the air fryer basket. If necessary, cook in batches to prevent crowding. Apply a thin layer of frying spray on the fries. Fries should be air-

fried for 15 to 20 minutes at 380°F (193°C), shaking the basket halfway through, or until they are crispy and golden brown. Depending on your air fryer type and the fries' thickness, the precise cooking time may change.

5. Sprinkle grated Parmesan cheese on heated fries immediately after cooking. Carefully toss fries to distribute melted cheese.

Serve:

➢ If preferred, garnish with freshly chopped parsley. Serve hot as a side dish or with your preferred dipping sauces.

NOTE:

➢ Halfway through the cooking process, you can lightly mist the fries with more cooking spray for even more crispiness.
➢ To add flavor, squeeze lemon juice or sprinkle additional Parmesan cheese before serving.

INGREDIENTS:

- ❖ 1 large eggplant
- ❖ 1/2 cup all-purpose flour
- ❖ 2 large eggs, beaten
- ❖ 1 cup panko breadcrumbs
- ❖ 1/4 cup grated Parmesan cheese
- ❖ 1/2 teaspoon garlic powder
- ❖ 1/2 teaspoon onion powder
- ❖ 1/2 teaspoon dried oregano or basil (optional)
- ❖ 1/4 teaspoon salt
- ❖ 1/4 teaspoon black pepper
- ❖ Cooking spray

INSTRUCTIONS:

1. Get the eggplant ready:
2. Clean and peel the eggplant (this step is optional, but it can help make the eggplant taste less bitter). Slice the eggplant into sticks or fries that are approximately half an inch thick.
3. Breading Station Setup: Assemble three shallow bowls for the breading station. Put the flour in the first bowl. Transfer the beaten eggs to the second bowl.
4. In the third bowl, mix panko breadcrumbs, grated Parmesan cheese, dried oregano or basil (if preferred), onion powder, garlic powder, and black pepper.
5. Cover each eggplant stick with flour and shake off excess to make breaded eggplant fries. Lean it over and drop

into beaten eggs. Spread the breadcrumb mixture over top and press gently to stick.

6. Pre-heat the air fryer for five minutes at 375°F (190°C).
7. Cook Eggplant Fries: Breaded fries should be in a single layer in the air fryer basket. To help them crisp up, give them a light cooking spray application. Fries should be cooked for 10 to 12 minutes at 375°F (190°C), rotating them halfway through, or until they are crispy and golden brown.

To serve, take the eggplant fries out of the air fryer and let them to cool down a little. Serve hot with your preferred ranch, marinara, or hot aioli for dipping.

NOTE:

➤ You may double-coat the eggplant fries by repeating the breadcrumb and egg procedures for even more crunch.
➤ Verify that the eggplant fries are equally coated in the breadcrumb mixture and are not packed too tightly in the air fryer basket if they are too soft.

INGREDIENTS:

- ❖ 4 large russet potatoes
- ❖ 2 tablespoons olive oil
- ❖ 1 teaspoon salt
- ❖ 1/2 teaspoon black pepper
- ❖ 1/2 teaspoon smoked paprika
- ❖ 1/2 teaspoon ground cinnamon
- ❖ 1/2 teaspoon chili powder
- ❖ 1/4 teaspoon cayenne pepper (adjust to taste for spiciness)
- ❖ 2 tablespoons brown sugar
- ❖ Cooking spray

INSTRUCTIONS:

1. Wash and scrape potatoes to prepare. Cut them into 1/4-1/2-inch wedges or fries.
2. Toss the potato strips in olive oil in a big bowl until they are equally covered. This is how you season the potatoes. Brown sugar, chili powder, black pepper, smoked paprika, ground cinnamon, and cayenne pepper (if using) should be added. To guarantee that the spice is dispersed equally, toss thoroughly.
3. Heat the Air Fryer: Set the air fryer's temperature for five minutes to 380°F (193°C).
4. Cook the Fries: Spread out the seasoned potato strips in a single layer into the air fryer basket. If necessary, cook in batches to prevent crowding. Apply a thin layer of frying spray on the fries. Fries should be air-fried for 15–20

minutes at 380°F (193°C), shaking the basket halfway through, until crispy and golden brown.

Air fryer fries should be cooled before serving. Serve hot as a side or with your favorite sauces.

NOTE:

➢ The amount of cayenne pepper depends on your heat preference. You can remove it for a gentler version.
➢ Before serving, you can pour some honey or maple syrup over the fries for an added touch of sweetness.
➢ For optimal flavor, make sure the fries are evenly covered in seasoning.

INGREDIENTS:

- ❖ 4 large russet potatoes
- ❖ 2 tablespoons olive oil
- ❖ 1 teaspoon salt
- ❖ 1/2 teaspoon black pepper
- ❖ 1/2 teaspoon garlic powder
- ❖ 1/2 teaspoon dried rosemary/thyme (optional)
- ❖ Cooking spray

For the Garlic Aioli:

- ❖ 1/2 cup mayonnaise
- ❖ 2 cloves garlic, minced
- ❖ 1 tablespoon lemon juice
- ❖ 1/2 teaspoon Dijon mustard
- ❖ Salt and black pepper to taste

INSTRUCTIONS:

1. Wash and scrape potatoes to prepare. Cut them into 1/4-1/2-inch wedges or fries.
2. Toss the potato strips in olive oil in a big bowl until they are equally covered. This is how you season the potatoes. Incorporate the salt, black pepper, garlic powder, and, if desired, dried thyme or rosemary. To guarantee that the spice is dispersed equally, toss thoroughly.
3. Heat the Air Fryer: Set the air fryer's temperature for five minutes to 380°F (193°C).

4. Cook the Fries: Spread out the seasoned potato strips in a single layer into the air fryer basket. If necessary, cook in batches to prevent crowding. Apply a thin layer of frying spray on the fries. Fries should be air-fried for 15 to 20 minutes at 380°F (193°C), shaking the basket halfway through, or until they are crispy and golden brown.
5. To make the Garlic Aioli, put the mayonnaise, lemon juice, minced garlic, Dijon mustard, black pepper, and salt in a small bowl. Blend until completely smooth. Taste and adjust the seasoning.

To serve, take the fries out of the air fryer and allow them to cool a little. Serve hot, with the garlicky aioli available for dipping on the side.

NOTE:

➢ You can add more minced garlic to the aioli for a deeper garlic taste.
➢ Add a little extra lemon juice or Dijon mustard if you like your aioli to have a little more tang.
➢ You may prepare the garlic aioli in advance and keep it in the fridge for up to a week.

INGREDIENTS:

- ❖ 4 large russet potatoes
- ❖ 2 tablespoons olive oil
- ❖ 1 teaspoon salt
- ❖ 1/2 teaspoon black pepper
- ❖ 1 teaspoon garlic powder
- ❖ 1/2 teaspoon paprika
- ❖ 1/2 cup shredded cheddar cheese
- ❖ 1/4 cup crumbled cooked bacon (4 pieces)
- ❖ 2 tablespoons chopped green onions
- ❖ Sour cream (optional, for serving)

INSTRUCTIONS:

1. Wash and scrape potatoes to prepare. Cut them into 1/4-1/2-inch wedges or fries.
2. Stir the potato strips in olive oil in a large basin until evenly coated. Here's how to season potatoes.
3. You can add paprika, black pepper, garlic powder, and salt. Toss well to evenly distribute the seasonings.
4. For five minutes, preh
5. eat the Air Fryer to 380°F (193°C).
6. Cook the Fries: Spread out the seasoned potato strips in a single layer into the air fryer basket. If necessary, cook in batches to prevent crowding. Apply a thin layer of frying spray on the fries. Fries should be air-fried for 15 to 20 minutes at 380°F (193°C), shaking the basket halfway through, or until they are crispy and golden brown.

7. Add Cheese and Bacon: After the fries are done cooking, top them with a handful of shredded cheddar cheese. Put the basket back in the air fryer and cook for a further two to three minutes, or until the cheese is melted and bubbling, at 380°F/193°C. Take out of the air fryer and top with chopped green onions and crumbled bacon.

Serve: If desired, top the hot loaded fries with a dollop of sour cream on the side.

NOTE:

- ➢ You can top the loaded fries with a sprinkling of paprika or a drizzle of spicy sauce for more flavor.
- ➢ Try pepper jack or mozzarella for a change.
- ➢ For the best texture and flavor, make sure the bacon is crispy before adding it to the fries.

40. CRISPY BRUSSELS SPROUTS

INGREDIENTS:

- ❖ 1 pound Brussels sprouts
- ❖ 2 tablespoons olive oil
- ❖ 1/2 teaspoon salt
- ❖ 1/4 teaspoon black pepper
- ❖ 1/2 teaspoon garlic powder
- ❖ 1/2 teaspoon onion powder
- ❖ 1/2 teaspoon smoked paprika (optional for extra flavor)

INSTRUCTIONS:

1. Trim Brussels sprout ends and remove yellow or broken leaves. If the Brussels sprouts are large, cut them in half lengthwise; if the
2. Leave small ones whole.
3. In a large bowl, evenly coat Brussels sprouts with olive oil. How to season sprouts. If using, add smoked paprika, salt, black pepper, onion powder, and garlic powder. Toss well to distribute spice evenly.
4. Heat the air fryer.
5. Preheat air fryer to 375°F (190°C) for 5 minutes.
6. Brussels sprout preparation:
7. Spread out the seasoned Brussels sprouts in a single layer into the air fryer basket. To prevent crowding, cook in separate batches. Cooking spray in a thin layer over Brussels sprouts. Air fry Brussels sprouts for 15 to 18

minutes at 375°F (190°C), shaking the basket halfway through, to get them crispy and golden brown.

8. Garnish Brussels sprouts with Parmesan cheese during the final two to three minutes of cooking, if desired. Melt and crisp the cheese.

Remove Brussels sprouts from air fryer and cool before serving. Serve hot as a snack or side.

NOTE:

➢ To enhance flavor, add balsamic glaze or lemon juice before serving.
➢ Add red pepper flakes to Brussels sprouts before cooking to make them spicier.

INGREDIENTS:

- ❖ 2 medium zucchinis
- ❖ 1/2 cup all-purpose flour
- ❖ 2 large eggs, beaten
- ❖ 1 cup panko breadcrumbs
- ❖ 1/2 cup grated Parmesan cheese
- ❖ 1/2 teaspoon garlic powder
- ❖ 1/2 teaspoon onion powder
- ❖ 1/2 teaspoon dried Italian seasoning (optional)
- ❖ 1/4 teaspoon salt
- ❖ 1/4 teaspoon black pepper
- ❖ Cooking spray

INSTRUCTIONS:

1. Get the zucchini ready:
2. Straw the zucchini and pat dry. Slice them into thin rounds that are about 1/4 inch thick after cutting off the ends.
3. Breading Station Setup: Assemble three shallow bowls for the breading station. Put the flour in the first bowl. Transfer the beaten eggs to the second bowl. Combine the panko breadcrumbs, grated Parmesan cheese, dried Italian seasoning (if using), onion and garlic powders, salt, and black pepper in the third bowl.
4. To make zucchini chips, bread each slice by dredging it in flour and shaking off any excess. Lean it over and drop it into the beaten eggs. Next, cover it with the breadcrumb mixture and gently press it to cling.

5. The air fryer should be preheated for five minutes to 375°F (190°C).
6. To cook the zucchini chips, place the breaded slices of zucchini in a single layer in the air fryer basket.
7. To make them crispier, lightly mist them with cooking spray. Flip the chips halfway through after 8 to 10 minutes at 375°F (190°C), so transforming them from soft to crispy and golden brown.

NOTE:

➢ *Evenly and loosely arrang*e zucchini slices in the air fryer basket for optimum crispiness.
➢ For a kick, add cayenne or red pepper flakes to breadcrumbs.

42. BALSAMIC GLAZED CARROTS

INGREDIENTS:

- ❖ 1 lb baby carrots (or 4 large peeled and sliced carrot sticks)
- ❖ 2 tablespoons olive oil
- ❖ 2 tablespoons balsamic vinegar
- ❖ 1 tablespoon honey or maple syrup
- ❖ 1/2 teaspoon garlic powder
- ❖ Dried thyme or rosemary, 1/2 teaspoon
- ❖ 1/4 teaspoon salt
- ❖ 1/4 teaspoon black pepper
- ❖ Fresh parsley, chopped (optional, for garnish)

INSTRUCTIONS:

1. Prepare the Carrots: Peel and cut into 1/4-inch-thick sticks, if using large carrots. If you're using baby carrots, you may either chop them in half lengthwise or leave them whole.
2. Toss the carrots in olive oil in a big bowl until they are equally covered. This is how you season the carrots. Add the garlic powder, dried thyme or rosemary (if using), balsamic vinegar, honey or maple syrup, salt, and black pepper. Make sure the glaze and spice are equally spread by giving it a good toss.
3. Heat the Air Fryer: Set the air fryer's temperature for five minutes to 380°F (193°C).
4. Cook the Carrots: Spread out the seasoned carrots in a single layer into the air fryer basket. If necessary, cook in batches to prevent crowding. To help them caramelize,

give them a quick spritz with cooking spray. Carrots should be air-fried for 15 to 18 minutes at 380°F (193°C), shaking the basket halfway through, or until they are soft and starting to caramelize.

To serve, take the carrots out of the air fryer and give them a little time to cool. If desired, garnish with freshly chopped parsley. Serve hot as an accompaniment.

NOTE:

- ➢ Reduce the balsamic vinegar and honey/maple syrup in a small skillet over medium heat until it thickens, then toss in the carrots for a deeper coating.
- ➢ Depending on the model of your air fryer and the thickness of the carrot chunks, adjust the cooking time.

INGREDIENTS:

- ❖ 1 pound trimmed, rinsed fresh green beans
- ❖ melted 2 teaspoons unsalted butter
- ❖ 3 cloves garlic, minced
- ❖ 1/2 tsp salt
- ❖ 1/4 teaspoon ground pepper
- ❖ 1/4 teaspoon of hot, crushed red pepper flakes
- ❖ Not required: One tsp carefully shredded Parmigiano
- ❖ Garnish optional
- ❖ : One tsp freshly picked parsley

INSTRUCTION:

1. To prepare the green beans, trim the ends and wash them well. Pat them dry with a paper towel.
2. In a large bowl, mix green beans, melted butter, minced garlic, salt, black pepper, and crushed red pepper flakes (if using).
3. Ensure that the coating of the green beans is uniform.
4. For five minutes, preheat the air fryer to 375°F (190°C).
5. Cook Green Beans: Spread the seasoned green beans out in a single layer inside the air fryer basket. To prevent crowding, cook in separate batches. Coat green beans gently with cooking spray. Green beans should be air-fried for 8 to 10 minutes at 375°F (190°C), shaking the basket halfway through, until they are soft and
6. beginning to crisp up.

To serve, take out the air-fried green beans and allow them to cool down a little. If desired, garnish with freshly chopped parsley. Serve hot as an accompaniment.

NOTE:

- ➢ Add another minced garlic clove for flavor.
- ➢ Before serving, you can squeeze a little lemon juice over the green beans if you like a stronger flavor.
- ➢ Adjust the cooking time Depending on the air fryer's model and the green beans' thickness.

INGREDIENTS:

- ❖ 1 pound fresh asparagus spears, trimmed
- ❖ 2 tablespoons olive oil
- ❖ 1/2 teaspoon salt
- ❖ 1/4 teaspoon black pepper
- ❖ 1/4 teaspoon garlic powder
- ❖ 1/4 teaspoon onion powder
- ❖ 1/4 teaspoon lemon zest (optional, for a fresh flavor)
- ❖ 1 tablespoon grated Parmesan cheese (optional for added flavor)
- ❖ 1 tablespoon lemon juice (optional for added brightness)

INSTRUCTIONS:

1. Get the asparagus ready:
2. Remove the rough ends from the asparagus spears and wash and trim them.
3. Stir olive oil into asparagus in a large basin. How asparagus is seasoned. You can add salt, black pepper, onion powder, garlic powder, and lemon zest. Stir to evenly distribute spices.
4. Preheat air fryer to 375°F (190°C) for 5 minutes.
5. Cook seasoned spears in a single layer in the air fryer basket. Avoid crowding by cooking in batches. If desired, spray cooking spray thinly. Steam-fry asparagus at 375°F (190°C) for 8–10 minutes, turning the basket halfway through, until tender and crackling.

6. Optional: Parmesan cheese In the last two minutes of cooking, sprinkle Parmesan cheese on asparagus. Let it melt and crisp.

To serve, take the asparagus out of the air fryer and allow it to cool down a little. If preferred, drizzle with lemon juice and serve warm.

NOTE:

➢ A pinch of red pepper flakes adds spice and flavor.
➢ Air fryer model and asparagus stem thickness effect cooking time.
➢ Add herbs, cumin, or paprika to taste.

INGREDIENTS:

- ❖ Cleaning and trimming 1 pound button or cremini mushrooms
- ❖ 2 tablespoons olive oil
- ❖ 1/2 teaspoon salt
- ❖ 1/4 teaspoon black pepper
- ❖ 1/2 teaspoon dried thyme
- ❖ 1/2 teaspoon dried rosemary
- ❖ 1/2 teaspoon garlic powder
- ❖ 1/2 teaspoon onion powder
- ❖ Chopped fresh parsley (optional garnish): 1 tbsp

INSTRUCTIONS:

1. Remove dirt from mushrooms with a damp paper towel. Remove stems if needed. If considerable, quarter or half the mushrooms.
2. Toss mushrooms in a large bowl of olive oil to coat. Add onion, garlic, dried thyme, rosemary, and black pepper powders. Toss mushrooms to evenly season.
3. Pre-heat the
4. air fryer for five minutes at 375°F (190°C).
5. Cook mushrooms: Place seasoned mushrooms in the air fryer basket in a single layer. Avoid crowding by cooking in batches. If desired, lightly coat with cooking spray. Shake the basket midway during the air fry cycle and cook the mushrooms for 10–12 minutes at 375°F (190°C) until tender and golden.

Remove the mushrooms from the air fryer and cool before serving. Serve warm, garnished if preferred with finely chopped fresh parsley.

NOTE:

➢ To enhance flavor, add lemon juice or balsamic vinegar just before serving.
➢ Adjust frying time based on air fryer model and mushroom size.
➢ Oregano and basil are also options, depending on your taste.

46. MAPLE GLAZED BUTTERNUT SQUASH

INGREDIENTS:

- ❖ 1 small butternut squash (about 2 pounds), peeled, seeded, and cut into 1-inch cubes
- ❖ 2 tablespoons olive oil
- ❖ 2 tablespoons pure maple syrup
- ❖ 1 tablespoon balsamic vinegar
- ❖ 1/2 teaspoon ground cinnamon
- ❖ 1/4 teaspoon ground nutmeg
- ❖ 1/2 teaspoon salt
- ❖ 1/4 teaspoon black pepper
- ❖ 1/4 cup of walnuts or pecans, chopped finely
- ❖ Garnish with fresh thyme or parsley, if preferred.

INSTRUCTIONS:

1. Using a vegetable peeler, start preparing the butternut squash by peeling it. Slice the flesh into one-inch cubes after trimming the ends and taking out the seeds.
2. Make careful to thoroughly coat the butternut squash cubes by tossing them in a large basin of olive oil. This is the correct way to season the squash. Combine the cinnamon, black pepper, maple syrup, and balsamic vinegar with the ground nutmeg. Make sure the squash is evenly coated by giving it a good toss.
3. Five minutes will let the air fryer reach 380°F (193°C).
4. Prep the squash: Place seasoned butternut squash cubes in the air fryer basket in a single layer. Avoid crowding by cooking in batches. Try spritzing it with cooking spray.

Squash should be air-fried for 15–20 minutes at 380°F (193°C), shaking the basket halfway through, until tender and caramelized.

5. Optional Nut Addition: If adding nuts, boil the squash for a further three to five minutes. As a result, the nuts will roast and become crispy.

6. Before serving, let the butternut squash cool slightly after removing it from the air fryer. Garnish with fresh thyme or parsley, if preferred. Present with heated portions.

NOTE:

➢ Vary the cooking time according to the type of your air fryer and the size of the butternut squash cubes.

➢ If you want to add a bit extra sweetness to the squash, you can drizzle it with some maple syrup right before serving.

➢ Make sure the squash pieces are coated uniformly and put in a single layer for best results.

INGREDIENTS:

- ❖ 1 pound broccoli florets (about 4 cups)
- ❖ 2 tablespoons olive oil
- ❖ 3 cloves garlic, minced
- ❖ 1 tablespoon lemon juice
- ❖ 1 teaspoon lemon zest
- ❖ 1/2 teaspoon salt
- ❖ 1/4 teaspoon black pepper
- ❖ For heat, add 1/4 teaspoon red pepper flakes.
- ❖ 1 tablespoon grated Parmesan cheese (optional for added flavor)
- ❖ Fresh lemon wedges (optional, for garnish)

INSTRUCTIONS:

1. Prepare the broccoli:
2. Wash and cut broccoli into bite-sized pieces. To absorb moisture, pat them dry with a paper towel.
3. Coat broccoli florets in olive oil in a big bowl prior to serving. Combine finely minced garlic, lemon zest and juice, salt, black pepper, and red pepper flakes—if desired. Toss broccoli to have consistent seasoning.
4. Pre-heat th
5. e air fryer for five minutes at 375°F (190°C).
6. Season the broccoli florets and place them in the air fryer basket in a single layer. Avoid crowding by cooking in batches. If desired, lightly coat with cooking spray. Air fry the broccoli for 8–10 minutes at 375°F (190°C), shaking

the basket halfway through, until soft and just starting to crisp along the edges.

7. Sprinkle Parmesan cheese over broccoli in the last two minutes of cooking. Let it melt and crunch.

Remove the broccoli from the air fryer and cool before serving. Add freshly sliced lemon slices if desired. Provide hot accompaniment.

NOTE:

➢ For taste, pour extra lemon juice over the broccoli before serving.

➢ Adjust cooking time based on broccoli floret size and air fryer type.

➢ Try adding soy sauce or smoked paprika for a unique taste.

INGREDIENTS:

- ❖ 1 pound broccoli florets (about 4 cups)
- ❖ 2 tablespoons olive oil
- ❖ 3 cloves garlic, minced
- ❖ 1 tablespoon lemon juice
- ❖ 1 teaspoon lemon zest
- ❖ 1/2 teaspoon salt
- ❖ 1/4 teaspoon black pepper
- ❖ Garnish with 1/4 teaspoon red pepper flakes for a little heat.
- ❖ 1 tablespoon grated Parmesan cheese (optional for added flavor)
- ❖ Fresh lemon wedges (optional, for garnish)

INSTRUCTIONS:

1. Prepare the broccoli:
2. Wash and cut broccoli into bite-sized pieces. To absorb moisture, pat them dry with a paper towel.
3. In a large bowl, stir broccoli in olive oil before serving. Mix in minced garlic, salt, black pepper, red pepper flakes, lemon zest, and juice. Season broccoli thoroughly.
4. For five minutes, the air fryer needs to be warmed to 375°F (190°C).
5. Cook the Broccoli: Place the seasoned broccoli florets in a single layer within the air fryer basket. If necessary, cook in batches to prevent crowding. If preferred, lightly mist with cooking spray. Air fry the broccoli for 8 to 10 minutes at 375°F (190°C), shaking the basket halfway

through or until it is soft and just beginning to crisp up around the edges.

6. Sprinkle Parmesan cheese over broccoli in the last two minutes of cooking. Let it melt and crunch.

To serve, remove the broccoli from the air fryer and allow it to cool slightly. If preferred, garnish with freshly cut lemon slices. Serve hot as an accompaniment.

NOTE:

- ➢ Before serving, squeeze more lemon juice over the broccoli for more flavor.
- ➢ Adjust cooking time based on broccoli floret size and air fryer type.
- ➢ For a unique touch, try experimenting with other ingredients, such as a dash of soy sauce or a pinch of smoked paprika.

INGREDIENTS:

- ❖ 1 pound fresh okra, trimmed and sliced into 1/4-inch thick rounds
- ❖ 1/2 cup all-purpose flour
- ❖ 1/2 cup buttermilk (or milk)
- ❖ 1 large egg
- ❖ 1 cup panko breadcrumbs
- ❖ 1/2 cup cornmeal
- ❖ 1/2 teaspoon garlic powder
- ❖ 1/2 teaspoon onion powder
- ❖ 1/2 teaspoon smoked paprika
- ❖ 1/4 teaspoon cayenne pepper (optional, for extra heat)
- ❖ 1/2 teaspoon salt
- ❖ 1/4 teaspoon black pepper
- ❖ Cooking spray

INSTRUCTIONS:

1. Prepare the okra:
2. Clean and chop okra. Circles 1/4 inch thick. Pat okra slices dry lightly with paper towels.
3. Setting up Breading Station: Prepare three shallow breading bowls. Place flour in the first bowl. Mix egg and buttermilk in a second bowl. In the third bowl, mix panko breadcrumbs, cornmeal, smoked paprika, onion and garlic powders, black pepper, and cayenne (if using).
4. Make Okra Bread: Dredge each slice in flour and shake off excess. Dip the buttermilk mixture to shake off excess.

Spread the breadcrumb mixture over top and press gently to stick.

5. Preheat Air Fryer to 380°F (193°C) for 5 minutes.
6. Okra Fries: Arrange the breaded okra segments in a single layer in an air fryer tray. In order to achieve a crispy texture, apply cooking spray to them gently. The okra should be crusty and golden brown after 10–12 minutes of air-frying, with the receptacle being shaken halfway through.
7. Turn the oven on high (380°F/193°C) to begin.

To serve, remove the fried okra and let it cool a little. Serve hot with your preferred dipping sauces, including hot sauce, ranch, or hot aioli.

NOTE:

➢ Before cooking, you can give the okra slices a quick mist with cooking spray for even more crunch.
➢ The okra slices' thickness and the type of air fryer you have will determine how long t
➢ hey should cook for.
➢ Feel free to incorporate extra spices or a small amount of dried herbs into the breadcrumb mixture for a personalized taste.

INGREDIENTS:

- ❖ 1-medium cauliflower, chopped into bite-sized florets
- ❖ 1/2 cup all-purpose flour
- ❖ 1/2 cup milk or buttermilk
- ❖ 1 large egg
- ❖ 1 cup shredded cheddar cheese
- ❖ 1/2 cup grated Parmesan cheese
- ❖ 1/2 teaspoon garlic powder
- ❖ 1/2 teaspoon onion powder
- ❖ 1/4 teaspoon smoked paprika (optional for extra flavor)
- ❖ 1/2 teaspoon salt
- ❖ 1/4 teaspoon black pepper
- ❖ Cooking spray

INSTRUCTIONS:

1. Prepare cauliflower:
2. Clean and dice cauliflower. Pat them dry with a paper towel.
3. Breading Station Setup: Assemble three shallow bowls for the breading station. Put the flour in the first bowl. Whisk the egg and the milk (or buttermilk) in the second bowl. Combine the shredded cheddar and grated Parmesan cheeses, salt, black pepper, onion and garlic powders, and smoked paprika, if using, in the third bowl.
4. Bread the cauliflower by brushing off any excess flour after dredging each floret in the flour. Lean it into the milk mixture and let any surplus run-off. Next, cover it with the cheese mixture and gently press it to stick.

5. For the first five minutes, heat the air fryer up to 375°F/190°C.
6. Breaded cauliflower bites should be placed in the air fryer basket in a single layer. Lightly spray them with cooking spray to crisp them up. After 12–15 minutes of air-frying at 375°F (190°C), shaking the basket halfway through, the cauliflower bites should be crispy and golden brown.

To serve, take the cheese-filled cauliflower pieces out of the air fryer and allow them to cool down a little. Serve hot with your preferred ranch or marinara dipping sauces.

NOTE:

➤ Before cooking, you may give the cauliflower bites a quick mist with cooking spray for even more crunch.
➤ Adjust cooking time based on cauliflower size and air fryer type.
➤ Try experimenting with other cheeses, or add a small dash of cayenne pepper for some heat.

INGREDIENTS:

- ❖ Adjust cooking time based on cauliflower size and air fryer type.
- ❖ 2 tablespoons olive oil
- ❖ 1 teaspoon smoked paprika
- ❖ 1/2 teaspoon ground cumin
- ❖ 1/2 teaspoon chili powder
- ❖ 1/4 teaspoon cayenne pepper (optional, for extra heat)
- ❖ 1/2 teaspoon garlic powder
- ❖ 1/2 teaspoon onion powder
- ❖ 1/2 teaspoon salt
- ❖ 1/4 teaspoon black pepper
- ❖ Fresh cilantro or parsley (optional, for garnish)

INSTRUCTIONS:

1. To prepare the sweet potatoes, peel them and cut them into one-inch cubes. P pat the cubes dry using a paper towel to eliminate any remaining moisture.
2. How to season sweet potatoes:
3. Dip sweet potato chunks in olive oil in a big bowl. Chile, ground cumin, smoked paprika, garlic, onion, black pepper, and cayenne should be used. Mix sweet potatoes with seasoning.
4. Heat t
5. he air fryer for five minutes at 400°F (200°C).
6. Sweet Potato Cooking: Place seasoned cubes in a single-layer air fryer basket. Cook in batches to avoid crowding.

7. Lightly spray with cooking spray. Air-fry sweet potatoes at 400°F (200°C) for 15–18 minutes until crispy and t
8. ender, shaking the basket midway.
9. Let air-fried sweet potato cubes cool before serving. Add fresh parsley or cilantro. Serve hot as a bite or side.

NOTE:

➤ For extra crunch, sprinkle sweet potato cubes with cooking spray before frying.
➤ Adjust cooking time based on air fryer kind and sweet potato cube size.
➤ Try adding paprika or turmeric for additional flavor. You can squeeze lime juice before serving.

INGREDIENTS:

- ❖ Core and strip 3 large any-color bell peppers.
- ❖ 2 tablespoons olive oil
- ❖ 1/2 teaspoon salt
- ❖ 1/4 teaspoon black pepper
- ❖ 1/2 teaspoon garlic powder
- ❖ 1/2 teaspoon onion powder
- ❖ 1/4 teaspoon dried oregano or basil (optional)
- ❖ 1/4 teaspoon smoked paprika (optional)
- ❖ Fresh parsley or basil (optional, for garnish)

INSTRUCTIONS:

1. To prepare bell peppers, clean, core, and cut them into strips. To absorb moisture, pat them dry with a paper towel.
2. Spice up bell peppers:
3. In a large bowl, coat the bell pepper strips with olive oil.
4. Season with salt, pepper, ground garlic and onion, and spices. Mix the peppers with the season
5. ing until they are evenly coated.
6. After just five minutes of quick preheating at 375°F (190°C), the air fryer is ready to go.
7. In the air fryer basket, place seasoned bell pepper strips. Avert overcrowding by cooking in batches. Apply a thin layer of cooking spray if preferred. Shake the basket halfway during the 8-10 minutes of air frying at 375°F (190°C) to soften and gently brown *the peppers.*

Give the bell peppers a chance to cool down after being air-fried. Toss in some chopped fresh parsley or basil if you like. As a side, wrap, salad, or sandwich, or serve hot.

NOTE:

- ➤ Make sure to adjust the cooking time based on the type of your air fryer and the thickness of the bell pepper strips.
- ➤ Before serving, you can brush the peppers with a balsamic glaze for added flavor.
- ➤ For a more colorful dish, you may even use different colored bell peppers.

53. GARLIC PARMESAN ARTICHOKES

INGREDIENTS:

- ❖ 1 can (14 oz) artichoke hearts, drained and patted dry (or use fresh or frozen artichoke hearts if preferred)
- ❖ 2 tablespoons olive oil
- ❖ 3 cloves garlic, minced
- ❖ 1/4 cup grated Parmesan cheese
- ❖ 1/2 teaspoon dried oregano or thyme
- ❖ For heat, add 1/4 teaspoon crushed red pepper flakes.
- ❖ 1/2 teaspoon salt
- ❖ 1/4 teaspoon black pepper
- ❖ Fresh parsley or lemon wedges (optional, for garnish)

INSTRUCTIONS:

1. To prepare the artichokes, cut them into quarters and remove any tough outer leaves, whether using frozen or fresh artichoke hearts. Before using canned artichokes, make sure they are thoroughly rinsed and patted dry.
2. Thoroughly coat artichoke hearts in olive oil in a large bowl. How to season artichokes. Use crushed red pepper flakes, dried oregano (or thyme), grated Parmesan cheese, black pepper, and sliced garlic. Toss the artichokes to coat them equally with seasonings.
3. Preheat t
4. he air fryer for five minutes at 375°F (190°C).
5. Cook Artichokes: Place seasoned artichokes in the air fryer basket in a single layer. Cook in batches to avoid crowding. If desired, lightly coat with cooking spray. Shake the basket halfway during the air fry cycle, then

cook the artichokes for 10–12 minutes at 375°F (190°C) until crispy and golden brown.

Take the artichokes from the air fryer and let them cool before serving. Add lemon wedges or fresh parsley. Serve hot as a starter or side.

NOTE:

➢ Add extra Parmesan cheese to the artichokes for crunch in the last two minutes of cooking.
➢ Adjust the cooking time depending on your air fryer's model and the size and kind of artichoke hearts.
➢ For extra brightness, pour freshly squeezed lemon juice over the artichokes before serving.

54. HERB BUTTER CORN ON THE COB

INGREDIENT:

- ❖ 4 fresh corn cobs, husked and cleaned
- ❖ 1/2 cup unsalted butter, softened
- ❖ 2 tablespoons fresh parsley, finely chopped
- ❖ 1 tablespoon fresh chives, finely chopped
- ❖ 1/2 teaspoon dried or fresh thyme
- ❖ 1 clove garlic, minced
- ❖ 1/2 teaspoon salt
- ❖ 1/4 teaspoon black pepper
- ❖ 1/4 teaspoon paprika (optional, for color)
- ❖ Cooking spray

INSTRUCTIONS:

1. To make the Herb Butter, place the softened butter in a small bowl and thoroughly mix in the minced garlic, chopped chives, chopped parsley, thyme, salt, and black pepper (if used).
2. Get the corn ready:
3. After cleaning and husking the corn, remove all of the rough outer layers and silk.
4. Use a paper towel to dry the corn.
5. To season the corn, evenly distribute the herb butter over the cobs. To ensure the butter is well dispersed, use a brush or the back of a spoon.
6. Heat the Air Fryer: Set the air fryer's temperature to 380°F (193°C) for five minutes.
7. Cook the Corn: Fill the air fryer basket with buttered corn on the cob. If the corn cobs don't fit in your air fryer, you

might have to chop them in half. If preferred, lightly mist with cooking spray. Air-fried the corn at 380°F (193°C) for 12–15 minutes, rotating halfway through, until tender and slightly browned.

To serve, remove the corn from the air fryer and allow it to cool a little. If desired, serve hot with any additional herb butter on the side.

NOTE:

- ➢ Adjust the cooking time depending on the model of your air fryer and the size of the corn cobs.
- ➢ Before serving, drizzle the corn with Parmesan cheese or squeeze lime juice for more flavor.
- ➢ You can cook the corn for a little longer if you prefer it to be crispy but watch it closely to avoid burning.

INGREDIENTS:

- ❖ 1 large eggplant, sliced into thin rounds (about 1/8-inch thick)
- ❖ 2 tablespoons olive oil
- ❖ 1/2 cup all-purpose flour
- ❖ 1/2 teaspoon salt
- ❖ 1/4 teaspoon black pepper
- ❖ 1/2 teaspoon garlic powder
- ❖ 1/2 teaspoon onion powder
- ❖ 1/2 teaspoon paprika
- ❖ 1/4 teaspoon dried oregano or thyme
- ❖ 1/4 cup finely grated Parmesan (optional flavor)
- ❖ Cooking spray

INSTRUCTIONS:

1. Wash and cut eggplant into thin rings. Sprinkle some salt on a baking sheet or cloth and arrange the slices in a single layer. Let them sit for 20 minutes to remove moisture and bitterness. Pat slices dry with paper towels.
2. Turn eggplant slices in olive oil in a large dish till coated. How eggplant is seasoned.
3. Make the Breading Station: Mix flour, paprika, dried oregano (or thyme), salt, black pepper, and onion and garlic powder in a small bowl. Add Parmesan cheese to the flour mixture or sprinkle it on the chips.

4. Cover the eggplant: Coat each eggplant slice in the seasoned flour and shake off excess. To crisp slices in the air fryer, lightly coat them with cooking spray.
5. Preheat air fryer to 375°F (190°C) for 5 minutes.
6. In a single layer, place breaded eggplant slices in the air fryer basket. Batch cooking reduces crowding.
7. Bake chips at 375°F (190°C) for 8–10 minutes until golden brown and crispy. Flip halfway.

Serve:

➢ Take the eggplant chips out of the air fryer and let them cool a bit. Serve hot as a crispy snack or with your preferred dipping sauce.

NOTE:

➢ Adjust the cooking time depending on the type of your air fryer and the thickness of the eggplant slices.
➢ Ensure the eggplant slices in the air fryer basket are wholly coated and well-spaced for maximum crispiness.
➢ Try experimenting with other ingredients or adding a small amount of cayenne pepper for a spicy kick.

56. ROASTED ROOT VEGETABLES

INGREDIENTS:

- ❖ After peeling, dice two medium parsnips.
- ❖ Cut a medium sweet potato thinly.
- ❖ 1 medium red potato, cut into bite-sized pieces
- ❖ 1 tablespoon olive oil
- ❖ 1 teaspoon dried rosemary or thyme (or a mix of both)
- ❖ 1/2 teaspoon garlic powder
- ❖ 1/2 teaspoon onion powder
- ❖ 1/2 teaspoon smoked paprika (optional)
- ❖ 1/2 teaspoon salt
- ❖ 1/4 teaspoon black pepper
- ❖ Fresh parsley (optional, for garnish)

INSTRUCTIONS:

1. Get the veggies ready:
2. All the root veggies should be cleaned, peeled if needed, and chopped into bite-sized pieces. Use a paper towel to remove excess wetness.
3. Toss the vegetables in a big bowl with olive oil to coat them equally before adding seasonings. Add the onion, garlic, smoked paprika (if using), dried rosemary or thyme, salt, and black pepper. Give the veggies a good toss to ensure they are well-seasoned.
4. The air fryer should be preheated for five minutes to 400°F (200°C).
5. Prepare the Veggies:
6. Put the seasoned veggies in a single layer inside the air fryer basket. If necessary, cook in batches to prevent

crowding. If preferred, lightly mist with cooking spray. Vegetables should be air-fried for 15 to 20 minutes at 400°F (200°C), shaking the basket halfway through until soft and browned.

Serve:

➤ After air-frying, let the vegetables cool. Garnish with fresh parsley. Serve hot as a snack or side.

NOTE:

➤ Adjust cooking time based on vegetable size and air fryer type. The vegetables must be crispy on the outside and soft on the inside.
➤ Before serving, pour a little lemon juice over the vegetables or toss some grated Parmesan cheese for more flavor.

57. CRISPY CHICKPEAS

INGREDIENTS:

- ❖ Use 1 1/2 cups cooked chickpeas instead of 1 can (15 oz) that has been drained and rinsed.
- ❖ 1-2 tablespoons olive oil
- ❖ 1/2 teaspoon smoked paprika
- ❖ 1/2 teaspoon garlic powder
- ❖ 1/2 teaspoon onion powder
- ❖ 1/4 teaspoon ground cumin
- ❖ 1/4 teaspoon ground coriander
- ❖ 1/4 teaspoon salt
- ❖ 1/4 teaspoon black pepper
- ❖ 1/4 teaspoon cayenne pepper (optional, for extra heat)
- ❖ Fresh herbs (optional, for garnish)

INSTRUCTIONS:

1. To prepare the chickpeas, drain and rinse them. Using paper towels, carefully pat them dry to remove any remaining moisture. Peeling the chickpeas adds an added crispy texture, but it's unnecessary.
2. To season the chickpeas, toss them in a big bowl of olive oil until they are well covered. Add the ground cumin, coriander, garlic powder, onion powder, smoked paprika, salt, black pepper, and cayenne (if used). Please give the seasonings a good toss to ensure they coat the chickpeas evenly.
3. The air fryer should be preheated for five minutes to 400°F (200°C).

4. Cook the Chickpeas: Spread the seasoned chickpeas in a single layer inside the air fryer basket. If necessary, cook in batches to prevent crowding. If preferred, lightly mist with cooking spray. Shake the basket halfway through the 15–18-minute air fry period at 400°F (200°C) to get crispy, golden-brown chickpeas.

To serve, remove the air-fried crispy chickpeas and let them cool a little. If desired, garnish with fresh herbs. Serve as an appetizer, salad dressing, or crunchy snack.

NOTE:

➢ Adjust the cooking time depending on the model of your air fryer and the size and moisture level of the chickpeas.
➢ Before seasoning and cooking, ensure the chickpeas are dry for optimal results.
➢ Keep crispy chickpeas in an airtight container at room temperature to maintain their crispness.

INGREDIENT:

- ❖ 2 peeled and sliced into quarter-inch rounds, medium sweet potatoes
- ❖ 2 tablespoons olive oil
- ❖ 1/2 teaspoon paprika
- ❖ 1/2 teaspoon garlic powder
- ❖ 1/2 teaspoon onion powder
- ❖ 1/4 teaspoon ground cumin
- ❖ 1/4 teaspoon salt
- ❖ 1/4 teaspoon black pepper
- ❖ 1/4 teaspoon dried thyme or rosemary (optional)
- ❖ To garnish, add fresh parsley or sea salt.

INSTRUCTIONS:

1. Cut peeled sweet potatoes into quarter-inch rounds. To fry slices evenly, cut them to thickness.
2. Lightly dry them with a paper towel.
3. Stir
4. the sweet potato slices in a large dish to coat them with olive oil. Sweet potato seasoning
5. two potatoes. Add salt, garlic powder, onion powder, paprika, dried thyme or rosemary, and powdered cumin. Toss the slices in the spices to co
6. at them.
7. Start by preheating the air fryer: For five minutes, air fry at 380°F (193°C).
8. Saute the slices of sweet potato: Layer the air fryer basket with the seasoned slices. You might not be able to cook

them all at once in the basket. Apply a thin layer of cooking spray if preferred. After 12–15 minutes of air-frying at 380°F (193°C), flip the sweet potato slices halfway through to ensure even cooking. Cook until crisp and soft.

When serving, wait for the sweet potato slices that have been air-fried to cool. If you choose, you can garnish it with fresh parsley or Sea Salt. Enjoy hot as a companion or appetizer.

NOTE:

➢ Depending on the model of your air fryer and the thickness of the slices, adjust the cooking time. Cooking times may need to be extended for thicker slices.
➢ For maximum crispiness, make sure the sweet potato slices in the air fryer basket do not overlap. Cook, if needed, in batches.
➢ To suit your tastes, try experimenting with various spice mixtures.

INGREDIENTS:

- ❖ 1 lb Brussels sprouts, trimmed and halved
- ❖ 2 tablespoons olive oil
- ❖ 2 tablespoons honey
- ❖ 1 tablespoon Sriracha sauce (adjust to taste)
- ❖ 1 tablespoon soy sauce
- ❖ 1 clove garlic, minced
- ❖ 1/4 teaspoon salt
- ❖ 1/4 teaspoon black pepper
- ❖ 1/4 teaspoon sesame seeds (optional, for garnish)
- ❖ Garnish with cilantro or green onions.

INSTRUCTIONS:

1. Cut Brussels sprouts in half and trim ends. Keep them equal in size for even cooking. Dry them with paper towels.
2. Make the sauce by mixing honey, Sriracha, soy, and minced garlic in a small basin.
3. Spread olive oil on Brussels sprouts in a big bowl. Sprout seasoning. Toss sprouts in honey-Sriracha to cover evenly. Toss again with salt and black pepper.
4. Preheat the air fryer for five minutes at 375°F (190°C).
5. Brussels sprouts cook: One-layer seasoned Brussels sprouts in the air fryer basket. Cook in batches to avoid crowding.
6. Coat lightly with cooking spray.

7. Air-fry Brussels sprouts at 375°F (190°C) for 12–15 minutes until crispy and tender, shaking the basket midway.

Serve Brussels sprouts after cooling from the air fryer. If preferred, add cilantro, green onions, and sesame seeds. Serve hot as a starter or side.

NOTE:

➢ Adjust cooking time based on Brussels sprout size and air fryer kind. Bigger sprouts may sprout slower.
➢ Ensure the Brussels sprouts are arranged in a single layer in the air fryer basket for maximum crispiness.
➢ The amount of Sriracha can be changed to suit your heat tolerance. If you like a tastier taste, you can use less or no Sriracha.

60. SPICY GARLIC CAULIFLOWER

INGREDIENTS:

- ❖ 1-medium cauliflower, chopped into bite-sized florets
- ❖ 2 tablespoons olive oil
- ❖ 1 tablespoon soy sauce
- ❖ 1 tablespoon Sriracha sauce (adjust to taste)
- ❖ 3 cloves garlic, minced
- ❖ 1/2 teaspoon smoked paprika
- ❖ 1/2 teaspoon ground cumin
- ❖ 1/4 teaspoon cayenne pepper (optional, for extra heat)
- ❖ 1/2 teaspoon salt
- ❖ 1/4 teaspoon black pepper
- ❖ Garnish with cilantro or green onions.
- ❖ Lime wedges (optional for serving)

INSTRUCTIONS:

1. Prepare cauliflower:
2. Clean and dice cauliflower. A paper towel will absorb any residual wetness.
3. Make the marinade:
4. Mix olive oil, soy sauce, Sriracha sauce, smoked paprika, minced garlic, ground cumin, cayenne pepper (if using), salt, and black pepper in a big bowl.
5. Turn the cauliflower florets in the bowl to coat them evenly in marinade, then season with salt and pepper.
6. Pre-heat the air fryer for five minutes at 375°F (190°C).
7. Place the seasoned florets in a single layer within the air fryer basket to cook the cauliflower. If necessary, cook in batches to prevent crowding. If preferred, lightly mist

with cooking spray. Roast the cauliflower for 15 to 18 minutes at 375°F (190°C), shaking the basket halfway through or until the edges are crispy and the cauliflower is soft.

To serve, remove the cauliflower from the air fryer and allow it to cool slightly. If preferred, garnish with green onions or fresh cilantro. Toss with lime wedges for a zesty taste explosion.

NOTE:

- ➢ Adjust the cooking time depending on the type of your air fryer and the size of the cauliflower florets. Bigger florets may take a little longer.
- ➢ Ensure only a little cauliflower is in the air fryer basket for maximum crispiness.
- ➢ You can vary the degree of spiciness by varying the amount of Sriracha and pepper to suit your taste buds.

61. CINNAMON SUGAR DONUTS

INGREDIENTS:

For the Donuts:

- ❖ 1 cup all-purpose flour
- ❖ 1/2 cup granulated sugar
- ❖ 1 1/2 teaspoons baking powder
- ❖ 1/4 teaspoon salt
- ❖ 1/2 teaspoon ground cinnamon
- ❖ 1/2 cup milk
- ❖ 1/4 cup unsalted butter, melted
- ❖ 1 large egg
- ❖ 1/2 teaspoon vanilla extract

For the Cinnamon Sugar Coating:

- ❖ 1/4 cup granulated sugar
- ❖ 1 tablespoon ground cinnamon
- ❖ 2 tablespoons melted butter (for brushing)

INSTRUCTIONS:

1. In a large basin, mix flour, sugar, baking powder, salt, and ground cinnamon
2. for doughnut batter.
3. Mix egg, melted butter, milk, and vanilla in another bowl.
4. Mix wet and dry components. There will be many batters.

5. Heat the Air Fryer: For five minutes, heat to 350°F (175°C).
6. Air fryer-safe donut pans need light greasing. Make silicone molds or donut holes without a pan.
7. Put 3/4 batter in each donut. Smooth tops using spatula.
8. Making donuts in the air fryer basket? Avoid molds. Batch cooking may be needed.
9. Air-fry donuts 6–8 minutes at 350°F (175°C) until golden brown and toothpick-clean.Keep powdered sugar and cinnamon in a basin while donuts bake.
10. Prep powdered sugar and cinnamon in a separate bowl while donuts bake.
11. After air-frying, let the donuts cool. Moisten each donut with melted butter and dip or sprinkle cinnamon sugar on top.

Serve:

➢ Donuts can be served warm or at room temperature. Savor them as a sweet snack or with a cup of coffee at any time of day.

NOTE:

➢ Adjust cooking time based on donut size and air fryer type. Making donut holes or small donuts may be faster.
➢ You can also form the batter by hand into the shape of donuts if you don't have a donut pan, and then cook them like donut holes by changing the cooking time.

INGREDIENTS:

- ❖ Softened unsalted butter,
- ❖ 1/2 cup
- ❖ Granulated sugar--1/2 cup
- ❖ 1/2 cup packed brown sugar
- ❖ 1 large egg
- ❖ 1 teaspoon vanilla extract
- ❖ 1 1/4 cups all-purpose flour
- ❖ 1/2 teaspoon baking soda
- ❖ 1/4 teaspoon salt
- ❖ 1/2 cup chocolate chips (semi-sweet or milk chocolate)

INSTRUCTIONS:

1. In a large mixer, beat melted butter, brown sugar, and granulated sugar until frothy to produce dough.
2. Blend egg and vanilla until smooth.
3. In another basin, mix flour, baking soda, and salt.
4. Mix until just combined, then add dry ingredients slowly.
5. Add chocolate chips and fold.
6. Heat the Air Fryer: Heat the air fryer to 350°F (175°C) for five minutes.
7. Create Cookies: Use a tablespoon to scoop cookie dough into balls. Softly flatten balls to form cookies.
8. If your air fryer basket is tiny, bake the cookies in batches.
9. Prepare Cookies: Place cookies in the air fryer basket, spacing them apart to distribute. Whether you bake in batches depends on your air fryer size.

10. Air fried at 350°F (175°C) for 5–7 minutes until centers are firm and rims are golden brown. Cookies will firm as they cool.
11. Cool the Cookies:
12. Let air-fried cookies cool on a plate or wire rack for a few minutes before eating. They are mushy when removed but stiffen when chilled.

NOTE:

> ➢ Depending on the size of your cookies and the type of air fryer you have, adjust the cooking time. It could take longer to make thicker or bigger cookies.
> ➢ If you like softer cookies, remove them when they are still slightly soft in the center and just beginning to brown on the outside.
> ➢ If you'd like, you can also incorporate nuts or other mix-ins into the dough.

INGREDIENTS:

For the Apple Filling:

- ❖ 2 medium apples (Granny Smith or Honeycrisp work well), peeled, cored, and diced
- ❖ 1/4 cup granulated sugar
- ❖ 1 tablespoon lemon juice
- ❖ 1 teaspoon ground cinnamon
- ❖ 1/4 teaspoon ground nutmeg
- ❖ 1 tablespoon all-purpose flour (to thicken)

For the Pie Crust:

- ❖ 1 package refrigerated pie crusts (or homemade pie dough, rolled out to 1/8-inch thickness)
- ❖ 1 egg, beaten (for egg wash)
- ❖ 1 tablespoon granulated sugar (for sprinkling)
- ❖ 1/2 teaspoon ground cinnamon (for sprinkling)

INSTRUCTIONS:

1. To make the Apple Filling, put the diced apples, flour, granulated sugar, lemon juice, ground nutmeg, and cinnamon in a medium pot.
2. For 5–7 minutes, stir occasionally over medium heat until the liquid thickens and the apples soften. Remove the pan from heat and cool.
3. Prepare Pie Crust: Roll store-bought pie crusts on floured surfaces. Cut dough into squares, rectangles, or 4–6-inch circles using a cookie cutter or glass rim.

4. Put pie crusts on parchment.
5. Leave a border on both edges of each pie dough circle and lightly spoon apple filling onto one half to make hand pies.
6. Extra dough can be folded ove
7. r half-moon pies and rectangular hand pies.
8. Press or fork-crimp edges to seal.
9. The air fryer should be heated to 350°F (175°C) for five minutes.
10. Cook Hand Pies: Lightly brush tops with beaten egg. Add sugar and ground cinnamon.
11. Place hand pies in air fryer basket in single layer without touching. Batch cooking may be needed.
12. Hand pies should be air-fried for 8–10 minutes at 350°F (175°C) until crisp and golden brown.Cut and

serve hand pies after cooling. Eat them hot or.

NOTE:

➢ Fry time depends on hand pie size and air fryer model.
➢ Serve cooled hand pies with vanilla ice cream or powdered sugar and milk icing.

64. BANANA FRITTERS

INGREDIENTS:

- ❖ 2 ripe bananas, mashed
- ❖ 1/2 cup all-purpose flour
- ❖ 1/4 cup granulated sugar
- ❖ 1/2 teaspoon baking powder
- ❖ 1/4 teaspoon ground cinnamon
- ❖ 1/4 teaspoon vanilla extract
- ❖ A pinch of salt
- ❖ 1 large egg
- ❖ Cooking spray (for greasing)

INSTRUCTIONS:

1. To make the batter, mash the bananas, add the vanilla extract, and stir them together in a big bowl.
2. Mix the flour, baking powder, powdered cinnamon, and salt in a separate bowl.
3. Mix until just mixed, and add the dry ingredients to the wet ones.
4. Smoothly fold the beaten egg into the batter.
5. Heat the Air Fryer: Set the air fryer's temperature to 350°F (175°C) for five minutes.
6. Form the Fritters: Using a spoon or cookie scoop, spoon batter into the air fryer basket in heaping tablespoons. The batter can be formed into little mounds or fritters. To ensure consistent frying, make sure there is room between each fritter.
7. Cooking spray should be used sparingly on the fritters' tops.

8. Cook the Fritters: Air-fried the fritters for 8 to 10 minutes, or until they are cooked through and golden brown, at 350°F (175°C). To ensure equal browning, shake the basket halfway during the cooking process.

To serve, remove the fritters from the air fryer and let them cool slightly. You may eat them heated or at room temperature.

NOTE:

➤ For a sweeter fritter, put honey or powdered sugar over top before serving.
➤ Adjust cooking time based on fritter size and air fryer type. Bigger fritters take longer to cook.
➤ Add some chocolate chips, almonds, or dried fruit to the mixture for some added taste.

65. S'MORES BITES

INGREDIENTS:

- ❖ 1 package refrigerated pie crusts (or homemade pie dough, rolled out to 1/8-inch thickness)
- ❖ 1/2 cup graham cracker crumbs
- ❖ 1/4 cup granulated sugar
- ❖ 1/2 cup mini marshmallows
- ❖ 1/2 cup chocolate chips (semi-sweet or milk chocolate)
- ❖ 1 tablespoon melted butter (for brushing)

INSTRUCTIONS:

1. Pie Crust Preparation: On a surface dusted with flour, roll out the pie crusts. Cut the dough into small, two-inch-diameter squares or circles.
2. Get the Filling Ready:
3. Combine the granulated sugar and graham cracker crumbs in a small bowl. Then, apply the mixture to the inside of the bite-sized s'mores.
4. Put the S'mores Bites together:
5. Lightly sprinkle half of the dough squares or circles with the graham cracker mixture.
6. Add a few chocolate chips and miniature marshmallows on the top of each.
7. Press the edges of the second dough square or circular to secure it in place. For additional sealing, you can crimp the edges with a fork.
8. Heat the Air Fryer: Set the air fryer's temperature to 350°F (175°C) for five minutes.

9. Cook the S'mores bits: Use melted butter to brush the tops of the S'mores bits.
10. Place each bite in a single layer within the air fryer basket. Depending on your air fryer's size, you might have to cook in batches.
11. For five to seven minutes, or until the dough is golden brown and the marshmallows are melted and oozy, air fry at 350°F (175°C).

Serve:

➢ Let the S'mores bites cool a little before arranging them. They will be quite hot whenThey will be quite hot when they come out of the air fryer.

NOTE:

➢ Take care not to pack the s'mores bites too full, as the marshmallows may swell and spill when they cook.
➢ Before air-frying, you can add some sea salt to the top, and after cooking, you can drizzle some melted chocolate over it for more taste.
➢ Size of s'mores and air fryer model determine cooking time.

66. BLUEBERRY MUFFINS

INGREDIENTS:

- ❖ 1 1/2 cups all-purpose flour
- ❖ 1/2 cup granulated sugar
- ❖ 2 teaspoons baking powder
- ❖ 1/4 teaspoon salt
- ❖ 1/2 cup milk
- ❖ Quarter-cup melted butter or vegetable oil
- ❖ One hu
- ❖ ge egg
- ❖ 1 teaspoon vanilla extract
- ❖ 1 cup fresh or frozen blueberries
- ❖ Optional: 1 tablespoon granulated sugar (for topping)

INSTRUCTIONS:

1. In a large basin, mix flour, sugar, baking powder, and salt for muffin batter.
2. Mix the egg, milk, vanilla, and vegetable oil (or melted butter) in a separate basin.
3. Add wet and dry ingredients after quickly mixing. Few mergers.
4. Mix blueberries gently.
5. Before using, pre-heat the air fryer for 5 minutes at 330°F (165°C).
6. Line muffin pans: Line the air fryer basket with parchment or silicone. No lubrication needs basket liners.
7. Fill muffin pans two-thirds full with batter. Add granulated sugar for crunch and crisp.

8. One layer of muffin pans in the air fryer basket. Cooking in batches may be necessary for smaller fryers.
9. Bake the muffins for 10–12 minutes at 330°F (165°C) until a toothpick inserted in the middle comes out clean or the tops turn golden brown.
10. Air-fried muffins should cool on a wire rack.
11. How long muffins fry depends on their size and air fryer type. Larger liners or cups require longer baking.
12. Add lemon juice or zest to the batter.
13. Avoid adding frozen blueberries to batter to preserve color.
14. Mix the egg, milk, vanilla, and vegetable oil (or melted butter) in a separate basin.
15. After mixing properly, pour liquid mixture into dry mixture. Mixes little.
16. Mixing blueberries requires prudence.

Before using, pre-heat the air fryer for 5 minutes at 330°F (165°C).

17. Line muffin pans: Line the air fryer basket with silicone or parchment. Oiling the basket doesn't require liners.
18. Place batter equally in muffin pans. For crunch, sprinkle it with granulated sugar.
19. A muffin tin should be lined before air-frying. Cooking in batches may be necessary for smaller fryers
20. The recommended cook
21. ing time for the muffins in an air fryer is 10 to 12 minutes at 330°F, or 165°C. Put a toothpick in the center of each muffin and carefully remove it to check doneness. Also, color the muffin tops golden brown.

Air-fried muffins should cool on a wire rack.

NOTE:

- ➢ The size of the muffins and the instructions for your air fryer will determine how long they should cook for. Bake for a longer period of time if using larger linersor cups.
- ➢ A little lemon zest or juice can do wonders for the batter's flavor.
- ➢ To preserve the blueberry color, do not mix thawed blueberries with the batter.

INGREDIENTS:

For the Donuts:

- ❖ 1 cup all-purpose flour
- ❖ 1/2 cup granulated sugar
- ❖ 1/4 cup packed brown sugar
- ❖ 1 teaspoon baking powder
- ❖ 1/2 teaspoon baking soda
- ❖ 1/2 teaspoon ground cinnamon
- ❖ 1/4 teaspoon ground nutmeg
- ❖ 1/4 teaspoon ground ginger
- ❖ 1/4 teaspoon salt
- ❖ Pumpkin puree, 1/2 cup (not pie filling) from a can
- ❖ one-fourth cup liquid
- ❖ 1/4 cup vegetable oil
- ❖ 1 large egg
- ❖ 1/2 teaspoon vanilla extract

For the Cinnamon Sugar Coating:

- ❖ 1/4 cup granulated sugar
- ❖ 1 tablespoon ground cinnamon
- ❖ 2 tablespoons melted butter (for brushing)

INSTRUCTIONS:

1. To make the doughnut batter, combine the flour, brown sugar, granulated sugar, baking soda, baking powder, cinnamon, nutmeg, ginger, and salt in a sizable basin.
2. Combine pumpkin puree, milk, oil, egg, and vanilla in a separate bowl.
3. Mix wet and dry components after barely mixing. Lots of hitters await.
4. Start the air fryer at 350°F (175°C) for Five minutes.
5. Before making molds, lightly grease an air fryer-friendly donut pan. Silicone molds or donut holes work without pans.
6. Fill each donut pan three quarters with batter. Level surfaces with spatulas.
7. Before air-frying, fill donut molds. Microbaskets boil repeatedly.
8. Air-fried donuts for 8–10 minutes at 350°F/175°C until a
9. toothpick put into the middle comes out clean.
10. Mix cinnamon and powdered sugar in a bowl while donuts
11. bake. Coat donuts.
12. Take the air-fried donuts out and cool. After buttering, sprinkle cinnamon sugar on each donut.

You can serve donuts warm or room temperature. Have them with coffee or tea.

NOTE:

➢ Depending on the size of your donuts and the type of air fryer you have, adjust the cooking time. It could take longer to prepare larger or thicker donuts.

➢ Once the donuts are coated in cinnamon sugar, you can top them with chopped pecans or a drizzle of maple glaze for more taste.

INGREDIENTS:

For the Churros:

- ❖ 1 cup water
- ❖ 1/2 cup unsalted butter
- ❖ 1 tablespoon granulated sugar
- ❖ 1/4 teaspoon salt
- ❖ 1 cup all-purpose flour
- ❖ 2 large eggs
- ❖ 1 teaspoon vanilla extract
- ❖ Cooking spray (for greasing)

For the Cinnamon Sugar Coating:

- ❖ 1/2 cup granulated sugar
- ❖ 1 tablespoon ground cinnamon

For the Chocolate Sauce:

- ❖ 1/2 cup heavy cream
- ❖ 1/2 cup semisweet chocolate chips
- ❖ 1 tablespoon light corn syrup (optional for a glossy finish)
- ❖ 1/4 teaspoon vanilla extract

INSTRUCTIONS:

1. Churro Dough is made by boiling water, butter, sugar, and salt in a medium saucepan.
2. After boiling, remove from heat and whisk in flour to make a smooth dough.
3. Wait five minutes to cool the dough. Beat each egg carefully after adding. Mix in vanilla.
4. For five minutes, heat the air fryer to 375°F (190°C).
5. Carefully pipe four to six-inch churros into the air fryer basket or parchment paper without overlapping. Slice dough into sticks.
6. Prepare the churros: Spray a little frying sprayon them.
7. Single-layer the churros in the air fryer basket. Your air fryer size determines whether batch cooking is needed.
8. Bake at 375°F (190°C) for 8–10 minutes until golden brown and crispy.
9. While the churros are cooking, prepare the cinnamon sugar coating by combining the ground cinnamon and granulated sugar in a small basin.
10. To make the chocolate sauce, place the heavy cream in a small saucepan and heat it over medium heat until it simmers.
11. Take off the heat and toss in the chocolate chips, mixing until the chocolate has melted completely and the sauce has a smooth consistency. Stir in the vanilla essence and light corn syrup if using.
12. Coat the Churros: Take the cooked churros out of the air fryer and let them cool a little.
13. Coat each churro thoroughly by rolling it in the cinnamon sugar mixture.

Serve:

➤ Place the chocolate sauce on the side for dipping and serve the warm churros.

NOTE:

➤ Adjust frying time based on churros size and air fryer kind. Churros with more length or thickness may take longer.
➤ You may also serve the churros with a cream cheese dip or a caramel sauce for a unique twist.

69. MINI CHEESECAKES

INGREDIENTS:

For the Crust:

- ❖ 1 cup graham cracker crumbs
- ❖ 1/4 cup granulated sugar
- ❖ 1/4 cup unsalted butter, melted

For the Cheesecake Filling:

- ❖ 8 oz (225 g) cream cheese, softened
- ❖ 1/2 cup granulated sugar
- ❖ 1 teaspoon vanilla extract
- ❖ 2 large eggs
- ❖ 1/2 cup sour cream
- ❖ 1/4 cup heavy cream

For the Topping (optional):

- ❖ Fresh fruit, fruit compote, or chocolate ganache

INSTRUCTIONS:

1. For the crust, mix sugar, melted butter, and graham cracker crumbs in a medium bowl. Mixing sand and wet.
2. Fill silicone cupcake molds or liners with mixture.
3. Make cheesecake filling.
4. Beat softened cream cheese smooth in a large basin.
5. Add vanilla and sugar.
6. Stir well after adding each egg.
7. Sour cream and heavy cream should be added until smooth and creamy.

8. Heat the Air Fryer: Air-fried for five minutes at 320°F (160°C).
9. Fill Molds: Spoon or pipe cheesecake filling
10. into muffin liners 3/4 full.
11. Make Mini Cheesecakes:
12. Place muffin liners or filled molds in the air fryer basket. Your air fryer size may require batch cooking.
13. Air-fry 12–15 minutes at 320°F (160°C) until centers are set and tops are slightly puffed. Cheesecake centers should jiggle but hold.
14. Serve miniature cheesecakes 10 minutes after cooling in pans. Cool them on a wire rack.
15. Set cheesecakes overnight or in the fridge for two hours.
16. Garnish with fresh fruit, compote, or chocolate ganache before serving.

NOTE:

➢ Adapt cooking time to mini cheesecake size and air fryer type. Smaller cheesecakes cook faster than larger ones.
➢ Ensure the cream cheese is completely softened before combining to create a smoother texture.

INGREDIENTS:

For the Shortcake Bites:

- ❖ 1 cup all-purpose flour
- ❖ 1/4 cup granulated sugar
- ❖ 1 1/2 teaspoons baking powder
- ❖ 1/4 teaspoon salt
- ❖ 1/4 cup cold, diced unsalted butter
- ❖ 1/2 cup milk
- ❖ 1/2 teaspoon vanilla extract

For the Strawberry Filling:

- ❖ 1 cup fresh strawberries, hulled and chopped
- ❖ 2 tablespoons granulated sugar
- ❖ 1 tablespoon lemon juice

For the Whipped Cream:

- ❖ 1/2 cup heavy cream
- ❖ 2 tablespoons powdered sugar
- ❖ 1/2 teaspoon vanilla extract

INSTRUCTIONS:

1. Strawberry Filling: Cut strawberries and mix with lemon juice and granulated sugar in a small basin.
2. Let strawberries macerate for 15 minutes to release juices.
3. Mix flour, baking powder, granulated sugar, and salt in a large bowl to make Shortcake Bites.

4. Cut cold butter with a pastry cutter or fingertips until it resembles coarse crumbs.
5. Add milk and vanilla essence and whisk briefly. Don't merge too much.
6. On a floured surface, carefully press the dough into a 1/2-inch rectangle.
7. Cut dough into bite-sized pieces or shapes with a tiny cookie cutter.
8. Heat the Air Fryer: Heat the air fryer to 350°F (175°C) for five minutes.
9. Cook Shortcake pieces: Place parts in air fryer basket in a single layer. Your air fryer's size may require batch cooking.
10. Air-fry shortcake bits at 350°F (175°C) for 5–7 minutes until cooked through and golden brown.
11. Create soft peaks by whipping heavy cream, powdered sugar, and vanilla.
12. When the shortcake bites have cooled slightly, place a dollop of the macerated strawberries on top of each bite to assemble the Strawberry Shortcake Bites.
13. Place a dollop or a piping bag over the strawberries.

Serve:

➢ You can now serve the strawberry shortcake bites or store them in the fridge until you're ready to serve.

NOTE:

➢ An alternative would be to flavor the shortcake dough with a small amount of lemon zest.

➢ You can adjust the crumbliness of the shortcake bits by adding a small amount of extra milk to the dough. On the other hand, if the dough is excessively sticky, increase the flour a little.

➢ Before air-frying the shortcake bites, dust them with granulated sugar for extra texture and taste.

INGREDIENTS:

For the Crust:

- ❖ 1 cup all-purpose flour
- ❖ 1/4 cup granulated sugar
- ❖ 1/2 cup cold, diced unsalted butter
- ❖ 1/4 tsp salt
- ❖ For the Lemon Filling:
- ❖ 2 large eggs
- ❖ 1 cup granulated sugar
- ❖ 1/4 cup all-purpose flour
- ❖ half a cup of recently extracted lemon juice (about two lemons)
- ❖ Zest of 1 lemon
- ❖ 1/4 teaspoon salt

For Garnish (optional):

- ❖ Powdered sugar (for dusting)

INSTRUCTIONS:

1. A medium basin should contain flour, salt, and granulated sugar for the crust.
2. Cut cold butter into coarse crumbs using a pastry cutter or fingertips.
3. Press the mixture into a parchment-lined silicone mold or baking dish.
4. Heat air fryer.
5. Pre-heat the air fryer

6. for five minutes at 320°F (160°C).
7. Cook crust:
8. Cook the crust at 320°F (160°C) for 10 minutes in the air fryer basket till light golden. When creating lemon filling, let it cool.
9. Prepare lemon filling.
10. Mix eggs, granulated sugar, flour, lemon zest, juice, and salt in a medium bowl.
11. Include Lemon Filling:
12. Pour lemon filling over the half-cooked crust in the air fryer basket.
13. To prepare Lemon Bars
14. , return the basket to the air fryer and cook for 15-20 minutes at 320°F (160°C) until the sides are brown and the filling is set. Shake the center
15. to wobble.
16. Wait to cool completely in the pan before cutting the lemon bars into squares. Parchment paper helps removing bars from baking dishes easy.
17. Powdered sugar can be sprinkled before serving.

NOTE:

➤ Please adjust cooking time based on silicone mold or baking dish size and depth. A smaller, deeper dishmay take longer.
➤ Lemon zest or juice adds acidity.

INGREDIENTS:

For the Donuts:

- ❖ 1 cup all-purpose flour
- ❖ 1/4 cup granulated sugar
- ❖ 1 1/2 teaspoons baking powder
- ❖ 1/4 teaspoon salt
- ❖ 1/2 cup milk
- ❖ 1/4 cup unsalted butter, melted
- ❖ 1 large egg
- ❖ 1/2 teaspoon vanilla extract

For the Filling:

- ❖ 1/2 cup Nutella (or any chocolate hazelnut spread)

For the Cinnamon Sugar Coating (optional):

- ❖ 1/4 cup granulated sugar
- ❖ 1 tablespoon ground cinnamon
- ❖ 2 tablespoons melted butter (for brushing)

INSTRUCTIONS:

1. Mix flour, baking powder, granulated sugar, and salt in a large basin to create doughnuts.
2. In another bowl, beat egg, melted butter, milk, and vanilla.
3. Stir wet and dry ingredients until mixed. Will cost.
4. Heat the Air Fryer: Heat the air fryer to 350°F (175°C) for five minutes.

5. On a floured surface, carefully spread the dough to 1/2 inch thickness to make donuts.
6. Cut dough circles with glass or round cutters. Divide half the dough circles into donut shapes by cutting a smaller circle from the center with a tiny cutter or bottle cap.
7. Insert a tiny spoonful of Nutella into each dough round. Put the hole-filled donut on top and gently press the edges to close. Pinch or crimp the corners to stop Nutella from leaking.
8. Cook the Doughnuts: Spray the air fryer basket with frying spray or line it with parchment paper to prevent sticking.
9. Single-layer the filled donuts in the air fryer basket. You may need to cook in batches depending on your air fryer size.
10. Donuts should be cooked thoroughly and golden brown in 8–10 minutes at 350°F/175°C.
11. Optional: Coat Donuts Mix ground cinnamon and granulated sugar
12. in a small basin while donuts cook.
13. After air-frying, coat donuts with melted butter and roll in cinnamon-sugar. Sprinkle powdered sugar on them.

Cool the donuts before serving. Warm is best for appreciating them.

NOTE:

- ➢ Nutella may spill out of donuts if you load them too full during cooking.
- ➢ Before sealing the donuts, you can add a tiny pinch of sea salt to the Nutella, or after heating, you can drizzle some more Nutella on top for more taste.

73. APPLE CINNAMON CHIPS

INGREDIENTS:

- ❖ 2 big Granny Smith or Honeycrisp apples
- ❖ 1 tablespoon granulated sugar
- ❖ 1 teaspoon ground cinnamon
- ❖ 1/4 teaspoon ground nutmeg (optional)
- ❖ 1/2 teaspoon lemon juice
- ❖ Cooking spray

INSTRUCTIONS:

1. To prepare the apples, wash and core them. Slice the apples as thin as possible—ideally, about 1/8-inch thick—with a mandoline slicer or an extremely sharp knife. The chips will be crispier if the slices are thinner.
2. Assemble the mixture of cinnamon sugar:
3. Combine the powdered sugar, ground cinnamon, and ground nutmeg (if using) in a small bowl.
4. Get the apple slices ready.
5. Mix apple slices and lemon juice in a large bowl to prevent browning.
6. Sprinkle sugar and cinnamon equally on apple slices.
7. Heat the air fryer.
8. Preheat the air fryer for five minutes to 320°F (160°C).
9. Cook the Apple Chips: Place the apple slices in the air fryer basket in a single layer. Depending on the size of your air fryer, you might have to cook in batches.
10. To help the apple slices crisp up, lightly mist them with cooking spray.

11. For ten to fifteen minutes, or until the apple slices are crispy and golden brown, fry them at 320°F (160°C). To guarantee consistent cooking, check often and jiggle the basket every few minutes. It could take longer for thinner pieces.
12. Remove air-fried apple chips to a wire rack to cool before serving. They crisp up as they cool.
13. Storage: Keep refrigerated apple chips in an airtight jar at room temperature. It's best to consume them within a week.

NOTE:

➤ To avoid the apple chips from clinging to one another, spread them out in a single layer during frying.
➤ You can modify the amount of sugar and cinnamon to taste, aiming for a sweeter or spicier flavor. Add a small amount of cayenne pepper for a unique twist and a touch of fire.

INGREDIENTS:

- ❖ 1/2 cup unsalted butter
- ❖ 1 cup granulated sugar
- ❖ 2 large eggs
- ❖ 1 teaspoon vanilla extract
- ❖ 1/2 cup unsweetened cocoa powder
- ❖ 1/2 cup all-purpose flour
- ❖ 1/4 teaspoon salt
- ❖ 1/4 teaspoon baking powder
- ❖ Add 1/2 cup chocolate chips or pieces (optional).To avoid browning, combine apple slices and lemon juice in a large bowl.
- ❖ To obtain a uniform coating, toss the apple slices in the cinnamon sugar mixture.

INSTRUCTIONS:

1. To prepare the batter, melt the butter in a small saucepan over low heat or in a safe bowl that can be put in the microwave. Allow it to cool a little.
2. Melt the butter and the powdered sugar in a large bowl and whisk until smooth.
3. Whisk together the eggs and vanilla extract thoroughly after adding them.
4. After sifting in the cocoa powder, add the flour, baking powder, and salt. Mix until barely incorporated. Fold chocolate chunks or chips (if using) into the batter.
5. Heat the Air Fryer: Set the air fryer's temperature to 320°F (160°C) for five minutes.

6. To make the brownie bites, lightly grease or line a small muffin tin or silicone muffin cup with parchment paper.
7. The brownie batter should be poured or piped into the tiny muffin cups, filling each to about 3/4 of the way.
8. To prepare the brownie bites, set the silicone cups or small muffin tin in the air fryer basket. Depending on the capacity of your air fryer, you may need to cook in batches.
9. For 8 to 10 minutes, or until a toothpick inserted into the center comes out with a few wet crumbs, air fry at 320°F (160°C). The tops ought to be slightly cracked and set.
10. Chill and Present: Allow the brownie pieces to chill within the pan or cups for several minutes, then move them to a wire stand to cool thoroughly.
11. Optional Toppings: For an additional indulgent treat, you can add a little sea salt or pour melted chocolate over the cooled brownie bits before serving.

NOTE:

➤ Air fryer cooking times vary by model and size. Monitor brownie bits toward the end to avoid overbaking.
➤ If you like a fudgier texture, allow the brownie bits to set in the pan for a few minutes before transferring them to a wire rack.

INGREDIENTS:

For the Tart Shells:

- ❖ 1 cup all-purpose flour
- ❖ 1/4 cup granulated sugar
- ❖ 1/2 teaspoon baking powder
- ❖ 1/4tsp salt
- ❖ 1/2 cup cold, diced unsalted butter
- ❖ One huge egg yolk
- ❖ 1-2 tablespoons cold water (as needed)

For the Raspberry Filling:

- ❖ 1/2 cup raspberry jam or preserves

INSTRUCTIONS:

1. Combine flour, baking powder, granulated sugar, and salt in a large basin for tart dough.
2. Cut cold butter into coarse crumbsusing a pastry cutter or fingertips.
3. Include yolk. Mix dough with cold water. Not all water is needed.
4. After creating a disk, refrigerate dough for 30 minutes.
5. Heat the Air Fryer: Heat the air fryer to 350°F (175°C) for five minutes.
6. Spread the chilled dough to 1/8 inch thickness on a floured surface to make tart shells.
7. Cut dough circles with a round cutter or the rim of a glass. Press the dough rings into the cups of a mini muffin tin or

silicone muffin molds to form little tart shells. You can manually create the dough into tiny tartlets if you don't have a miniature muffin tin.

8. Fill each tart shell with a tiny tablespoon of raspberry jam.
9. Cook the Tarts: Place the prepared tart shells in the air fryer basket in a single layer. Depending on the size of your air fryer, you might have to cook in batches.
10. For 8 to 10 minutes, or until the tart shells are golden brown and the jam is bubbling, air fry at 350°F (175°C).
11. Cool and Serve: After a few minutes of cooling in the molds or tin, move the tarts to a wire rack to finish cooling.

NOTE:

➢ Before air-frying, you can decorate the jam by cutting out little shapes from leftover dough and placing them on top.
➢ If you want a slightly different filling, you can use different fruit preserves or jams or even combine fruit preserves with a small amount of cream cheese for a unique twist.

76. CHOCOLATE LAVA CAKES

INGREDIENTS:

- ❖ 1/2 cup (1 stick) unsalted butter
- ❖ 4 oz (115 g) semisweet or bittersweet chocolate, chopped
- ❖ 1 cup granulated sugar
- ❖ 2 large eggs
- ❖ 2 large egg yolks
- ❖ 1 teaspoon vanilla extract
- ❖ 1/2 cup all-purpose flour
- ❖ A pinch of salt
- ❖ Optional sprinkling sugar
- ❖ Serve with fresh berries or vanilla ice cream.

INSTRUCTIONS:

1. To make the cake mixture, heat butter and chopped chocolate for 30 seconds at a time until smooth and melted.
2. Add granulated sugar and stir.
3. Add eggs, egg yolks, and vanilla essence and mix well.
4. Mix flour and a pinch of salt until barely combined. Avoid overmix
5. ing.
6. Brush 4 ramekins with butter and flour or cocoa powder to prevent sticking. Even cooking spray works.
7. Fill
8. ramekins 3/4 full
9. with batter.
10. Preheat the air fryer for five minutes
11. at 350°F/175°C.

12. Place the ramekins in the air fryer basket in a single layer to cook the Lava Cakes. Your air fryer size may require batch cooking.
13. Air-fry at 350°F (175°C) for 10-12 minutes to harden the edges but maintain the centers soft and jiggly. Look for firm, slightly cracked tops.
14. Let lava cakes cool in ramekins for 1-2 minutes before serving. Invert onto serving plates after knife-releasing the edges.
15. Sprinkle powdered sugar and serve warm with berries or vanilla ice cream.

NOTE:

➢ Be careful not to overcook the lava cakes. For the classic lava cake experience, the centers should remain gooey and molten.
➢ For a variation, add a small piece of chocolate or a spoonful of Nutella in the center of each ramekin before baking for an extra gooey center.

INGREDIENTS:

- ❖ 2 cups shredded sweetened coconut
- ❖ 1/2 cup granulated sugar
- ❖ 2 large egg whites
- ❖ 1/4 teaspoon vanilla extract
- ❖ A pinch of salt
- ❖ Half a cup of semisweet chocolate chips, if desired for dipping

INSTRUCTIONS:

1. To make the Coconut Mixture, put the powdered sugar and shredded coconut in a big bowl.
2. The egg whites should be whisked with a bit of salt in a another bowl until stiff peaks form.
3. Once thoroughly blended, gently fold the beaten egg whites into the coconut mixture. Gently stir in the vanilla extract.
4. Lightly oil or line the air fryer basket with parchment paper to keep it from sticking
5. while you make the macaroons.
6.
7. Use a small cookie scoop or spoon to make coconut mounds in the air fryer basket. Air fryers vary in size, thus batch cooking may not be necessary.
8. Warm up the air fryer: Set the temperature to 320°F (160°C) for five minutes.
9. Directions for Preparing Food: The macaroons were air-fried for 8 to 10 minutes, or until the edges were golden

brown, at 320°F (160°C). The winners' color won't change all that much.

10. After the air fryer basket cools for a few minutes, place the macaroons on a wire rack to coolcompletely.

11. If desired, the semisweet chocolate chips can be melted for chocolate dipping by heating them in a microwave-safe bowl for 30 seconds at a time and stirring every 30 seconds.

12. After dipping the bottom of each macaroon into the melted chocolate, place the macaroons on a dish lined with parchment paper to set. As an alternative, you might cover the macaroon topping with chocolate.

➢ Serve: After the chocolate hardens, the macaroons are prepared for consumption. For up to a week, keep them at room temperature in an airtight jar.

NOTE:

➢ To avoid the chocolate melting, ensure the macaroons are completely cool before dipping them.

➢ You can flavor the coconut mixture further by including a small amount of almond essence or finely chopped almonds.

INGREDIENTS:

For the Peach Filling:

- ❖ 1 cup fresh or frozen peaches, diced
- ❖ 1/4 cup granulated sugar
- ❖ 1 tablespoon cornstarch
- ❖ 1/2 teaspoon lemon juice
- ❖ 1/2 teaspoon ground cinnamon

For the Biscuit Dough:

- ❖ 1 cup all-purpose flour
- ❖ 1/4 cup granulated sugar
- ❖ 1 1/2 teaspoons baking powder
- ❖ 1/4 teaspoon salt
- ❖ 1/4 cup cold, diced, unsalted butter
- ❖ 1/2 cup milk
- ❖ 1/2 teaspoon vanilla extract

For the Topping:

- ❖ 1 tablespoon granulated sugar
- ❖ 1/2 teaspoon ground cinnamon

INSTRUCTIONS:

1. Make the Peach Filling by mixing chopped peaches, cornstarch, granulated sugar, lemon juice, and ground cinnamon in a medium pot.
2. Stir often over medium heat for 5–7 minutes until the liquid thickens and the peaches are mushy. Let cool.
3. Prepare biscuit dough:
4. Blend flour, baking powder, granulated sugar, and salt in a large bowl.
5. Using a pastry cutter or fingertips, chop cold butter into coarse crumbs.
6. Whisk milk and vanilla briefly. Sticky dough.
7. Make Cobbler Peach Bites:
8. Roll biscuit dough to 1/4 inch thickness on a floured surface.
9. Slice dough circles with glass or circular cutters. Center each dough round with peach filling.
10. Cover the filling with the dough half-moon. Fork-crimp edges.
11. Heat the Air Fryer: Heat to 350°F (175°C)for 5 minutes.
12. To avoid sticking, lightly spray or line the air fryer basket with Peach Cobbler Bites.
13. Place one layer of bite-sized peach cobbler in an air fryer basket. Air fryers vary in size, so cook in batches.
14. Sprinkle powdered sugar and ground cinnamon on peach cobbler topsfrom a separate bowl.
15. Air fried until mixture bubbles and biscuit dough browns, 8–10 minutes at 350°F (175°C).
16. Relax Now: Chill peach cobbler before serving. Warm is better for appreciation.

NOTE:

➤ The peach filling should not be too hot when closing the dough to avoid issues in sealing.

➤ Add vanilla extract or nutmeg to the peach filling to flavor it.

INGREDIENTS:

For the Scones:

- ❖ 2 cups all-purpose flour
- ❖ 1/4 cup granulated sugar
- ❖ 1 tablespoon baking powder
- ❖ 1/4tsp salt
- ❖ 1/2 cup cold, diced, unsalted butter
- ❖ 1/2 cup chopped pecans
- ❖ 1/2 cup milk
- ❖ 1/4 cup pure maple syrup
- ❖ 1 large egg
- ❖ 1 teaspoon vanilla extract

For the Maple Glaze:

- ❖ 1/2 cup powdered sugar
- ❖ 2 tablespoons pure maple syrup
- ❖ 1-2 tablespoons milk (as needed for consistency)

INSTRUCTIONS:

1. In a large bowl, mix together the flour, baking powder, granulated sugar, and salt to produce the scone dough.
2. Cut cold butter into coarse crumbs using a pastry cutter or fingertips.
3. Stir in chopped pecans.
4. In another bowl, combine milk, egg, maple syrup, and vanilla.
5. Blend wet and dry ingredients. Low-stick dough.

6. For scones, lightly pat dough into a one-inch circle on floured surface.
7. Cut eight dough wedges with a pizza cutter or knife.
8. Heat the Air Fryer: For five minutes, the air fryer is heated to 350°F (175°C).
9. Make Scones: Line the air fryer basket with paper or
10. oil to prevent sticking.fries in the air fryer. Cook in batches based on your air fryer's capacity.
11. Air-fry the chicken at 400°F (200°C) for 10–12 minutes, flipping halfway, until opaque and golden brown. The required internal temperature is 165°F, or 74°C.
12. Air-fried single-layer scone wedges. Air fryers vary in size, so batch cook.
13. Air-fry scones till golden brown, 10–12 minutes at 350°F (175°C).
14. Mix powdered sugar, maple syrup, and milk in a small dish to make a drizzle-worthy mapl
15. e glaze while the scones cool.
16. Pour glaze on cooled scones.

Serve:

➢ Before serving, let the glaze solidify. Savor the warm or room-temperature scones.

NOTE:

➢ You can give the scone dough a dash of nutmeg or cinnamon for an even deeper taste.
➢ To keep the glaze from melting, make sure the scones are completely cold before glazing.

INGREDIENTS:

For the Topping:

- ❖ 1/4 cup unsalted butter
- ❖ 1/2 cup packed brown sugar
- ❖ 1 can (8 oz) pineapple rings, drained (reserve the juice)
- ❖ Maraschino cherries (optional)

For the Cake Batter:

- ❖ 1 cup all-purpose flour
- ❖ 1/2 cup granulated sugar
- ❖ 1 1/2 teaspoons baking powder
- ❖ 1/4 teaspoon salt
- ❖ 1/4 cup unsalted butter, softened
- ❖ 1/2 cup milk
- ❖ 1 large egg
- ❖ 1/2 teaspoon vanilla extract
- ❖ 1/4 cup pineapple juice (drained)

INSTRUCTIONS:

1. To prepare the topping, melt butter in a small saucepan over medium heat. Smoothly add brown sugar.
2. Brush butter and brown sugar on the bottom of an air fryer basket-compatible 6-inch round cake pan.
3. If using, arrange pineapple rings with maraschino cherries on top of the mixture.
4. For the cake batter, mix flour, baking powder, granulated sugar, and salt in a medium basin.

5. Beat softened butter in another bowl until smooth. Mix well after adding milk, egg, pineapple juice, and vanilla.
6. Add dry ingredients slowly and stir just until incorporated.
7. Build the
8. cake by gently pouring the cake batter over the pineapple rings in the pan.
9. The air fryer should be heated to 320°F (160°C) for 5 minutes.
10. Cook the cake pan in the air fryer basket. Whether you cook in batches depends on your air fryer size.
11. A toothpick inserted into the center should come out clean after 20–25 minutes of air-frying at 320°F (160°C). Cake must be set and golden brown.
12. Invert the cake after five minutes of cooling in the pan. Run a knife over the edges to loosen.
13. Carefully turn the cake onto a dish. The pineapple and caramel should be on top.

To serve, either warm or room temperature pineapple upside down cake should be served. It tastes great by itself or served with a dollop of vanilla ice cream.

NOTE:

➢ You can use a silicone mold or an oven-safe dish of a comparable size if you don't have a 6-inch round cake pan that fits your air fryer.
➢ Before pouring the batter over the pineapple, you might add a little cinnamon for taste.

81. STICKY ORANGE CHICKEN

INGREDIENTS:

For the Chicken:

- ❖ 1 lb chopped boneless, skinless chicken thighs or breasts
- ❖ 1/2 cup all-purpose flour
- ❖ 1/4 teaspoon salt
- ❖ 1/4 teaspoon black pepper
- ❖ 1 large egg
- ❖ 1/2 cup breadcrumbs (panko or regular)

For the Orange Sauce:

- ❖ 1/2 cup orange juice
- ❖ 1/4 cup soy sauce
- ❖ 1/4 cup granulated sugar
- ❖ 1 tablespoon rice vinegar
- ❖ 1 tablespoon cornstarch/2 tablespoons water (slurry)
- ❖ 1 teaspoon grated fresh ginger
- ❖ 2 cloves garlic, minced
- ❖ 1 teaspoon sesame oil
- ❖ Heat-optional 1/4 teaspoon crushed red pepper flakes

For Garnish (Optional):

- ❖ Sliced green onions
- ❖ Sesame seeds
- ❖ Orange zest

INSTRUCTIONS:

1. To prepare the chicken, combine the flour, salt, and pepper in a basin.
2. Beat the egg in a separate basin.
3. Coat the chicken pieces in breadcrumbs after dredging them in the flour mixture and dipping them into the beaten egg.
4. Put the breaded chicken pieces in the air fryer basket in a single layer. Cooking in batches could be necessary.
5. The air fryer should be preheated for five minutes to 400°F (200°C).
6. Cook the Chicken: Shake the air fryer basket halfway through cooking the chicken for 10–12 minutes at 400°F (200°C) until crispy and cooked through. At 165°F (74°C), check the interior temperature.
7. To create orange sauce, combine lime juice, sugar, rice vinegar, sesame oil, ginger, garlic, and soy sauce in a medium saucepan. Red pepper, crumbled.
8. Simmer on medium heat, stirring occasionally.
9. Thicken the sauce by stirring
10. in the cornstarch slurry while it simmers for two or three minutes. Shift the heat off.
11. Coat the Chicken: Using the orange sauce, toss the cooked chicken pieces until well coated.
12. Transfer the sticky orange chicken to a serving tray in order to serve. If preferred, garnish with orange zest, sesame seeds, and sliced green onions.

NOTE:

➢ You can fry the chicken for a few more minutes before smothering it in sauce for even more crunch.

➢ For a full dinner, serve the sticky orange chicken over noodles or steamed rice.

INGREDIENTS:

For the Chicken:

- ❖ One pound (450 grams) of skinless, boneless chicken thighs or breasts
- ❖ 1/2 cup all-purpose flour
- ❖ 1/2 teaspoon salt
- ❖ 1/4 teaspoon black pepper
- ❖ 1 large egg
- ❖ 1 cup breadcrumbs (panko or regular)
- ❖ 1/2 cup grated Parmesan cheese
- ❖ 1/2 cup marinara sauce
- ❖ 1 cup shredded mozzarella cheese
- ❖ Fresh basil or parsley for garnish (optional)

For the Sliders:

- ❖ 6-8 slider buns
- ❖ 2 tablespoons unsalted butter, melted
- ❖ Parmesan cheese, 1/4 cup, grated (for topping)

INSTRUCTIONS:

1. Get the chicken ready:
2. For five minutes, preheat the air fryer to 400°F (200°C).
3. Create a station for breading: Mix the flour, salt, and pepper in a bowl. In a separate bowl, whisk the egg.
4. A separate bowl
5. should have half a cup of grated Parmesan and breadcrumbs.

6. Before breading, dredge chicken in flour, beaten egg, and egg.
7. Flatten breaded chicken breasts in air fryer basket. Cook in batches
8. based on your air fryer's capacity.
9. Air-fry the chicken at 400°F (200°C) for 10–12 minutes, flipping halfway, until opaque and golden brown. The required internal temperature is 165°F, or 74°C.
10. Put the Sliders Together: While the chicken is cooking, grate some Parmesan cheese and brush the slider buns with melted butter. Toast the buns in the air fryer at 350°F/175°C for two to three minutes or until they are crispy and golden.
11. Once the chicken is cooked, top each piece with a few shredded mozzarella cheese and a dollop of marinara sauce. Return the cheese to the air fryer and continue cooking it for an additional two to three minutes or until it is bubbling and melted.
12. To assemble the sliders, place the cooked chicken pieces on the bottom halves of the toasted slider buns.
13. Top with the remaining bun.

Serve:

➢ Garnish with parsley or fresh basil, if preferred. Warm sliders should be served.

NOTE:

➢ You may top the sliders with a layer of sautéed spinach or a slice of fresh tomato for a little more flavor.

➢ Before serving, you can optionally top the melted mozzarella with a little more grated Parmesan cheese if you want a more classic Parmesan experience.

INGREDIENTS:

For the Chicken Patties:

- ❖ 1 lb (450 g) ground chicken
- ❖ 1/4 cup breadcrumbs (panko or regular)
- ❖ 1/4 cup grated Parmesan cheese
- ❖ 1 large egg
- ❖ 2 tablespoons mayonnaise
- ❖ 1 teaspoon garlic powder
- ❖ 1 teaspoon onion powder
- ❖ 1/2 teaspoon dried oregano
- ❖ 1/2 teaspoon dried basil
- ❖ 1/4 teaspoon salt
- ❖ 1/4 teaspoon black pepper

For Breading:

- ❖ 1/2 cup all-purpose flour
- ❖ 1 large egg, beaten
- ❖ 1 cup breadcrumbs (panko or regular)
- ❖ Cooking spray

For Serving:

- ❖ 4-6 hamburger buns
- ❖ Lettuce leaves
- ❖ Tomato slices
- ❖ Pickles
- ❖ Ketchup and mustard (optional)

INSTRUCTIONS:

1. Get the chicken patties ready.
2. Ground chicken, breadcrumbs, Parmesan cheese, egg, mayonnaise, onion and garlic powders, oregano, basil, salt, and pepper should all be combined in a big bowl. Blend until barely mixed. Take cautious not to blend too much.
3. Create the Patties:
4. Shape the ingredients into patties by dividing it into four to six equal portions. To guarantee consistent cooking, gently press them down.
5. Establish a breading station before breading the patties. Sort the flour into a shallow dish, then add the beaten egg and breadcrumbs to another dish.
6. Each chicken patty should first be coated in flour, dipped in beaten egg, and last covered in breadcrumbs. To make sure the breadcrumbs stick well, lightly press.
7. Heat the Air Fryer: Set the air fryer's temperature for five minutes to 380°F (190°C).
8. Cook the patties by lightly misting the cooking spray inside the air fryer basket.
9. Arrange the breaded patties in a single layer within the air fryer basket. Depending on how big your air fryer is, you might have to cook in batches.
10. For 10 to 12 minutes, air fried the patties at 380°F (190°C), turning them halfway through, or until they are cooked through and golden brown. A temperature of 165°F (74°C) should be reached internally.
11. As the chicken patties are frying, prepare the buns by toasting them in an air fryer set at 350°F/175°C for two to three minutes, or until they are crispy and brown.
12. Put the crispy chicken patties on the bottom halves of the toasted buns to assemble the burgers.

13. Add pickles, tomato slices, and lettuce on top. If desired, add mustard and ketchup.
14. The top half of the bun should be placed on top.

Serve:

➢ Warm up your favorite sides to go with the crispy chicken burgers.

NOTE:

➢ You can flavor the chicken mixture further by using some finely chopped fresh herbs or a small amount of spicy sauce.
➢ For the final two minutes of cooking, you can, if you'd like, place a slice of cheese on top of the chicken patties to melt it a little.

84. MANGO HABANERO CHICKEN WINGS

INGREDIENTS:

For the Chicken Wings:

- ❖ 2 lbs (900 g) chicken wings
- ❖ 1 tablespoon vegetable oil
- ❖ 1/2 teaspoon salt
- ❖ 1/2 teaspoon black pepper
- ❖ 1/2 teaspoon garlic powder
- ❖ 1/2 teaspoon onion powder

For the Mango Habanero Sauce:

- ❖ 1 cup mango chunks (fresh or frozen, thawed)
- ❖ 1-2 habanero peppers (adjust to taste), seeds removed
- ❖ 1/4 cup honey
- ❖ 1/4 cup orange juice
- ❖ 2 tablespoons rice vinegar
- ❖ 2 tablespoons soy sauce
- ❖ 1 tablespoon fresh lime juice
- ❖ 1 tablespoon grated fresh ginger
- ❖ 1 clove garlic, minced
- ❖ Salt to taste (if needed)

INSTRUCTIONS:

1. The chicken wings should be prepared by patting them dry with paper towels.
2. Toss the wings in a large basin with vegetable oil, salt, black pepper, onion powder, and garlic powder, being sure to coat them evenly.

3. Warm up the air fryer: For five minutes, set the air fryer's temperature to 380°F (190°C).
4. Cook the Chicken Wings: Put the chicken wings in the air fryer basket in a single layer. Depending on how big your air fryer is, you might have to cook in batches.
5. The wings should be air-fried for 20 to 25 minutes at 380°F (190°C), shaking the basket halfway through or until they are crispy and cooked through. A temperature of 165°F (74°C) should be reached internally.
6. To make the Mango Habanero Sauce, put the mango chunks, habanero chiles, honey, orange juice, rice vinegar, soy sauce, lime juice, ginger, and garlic in a food processor or blender.
7. Process till seamless. Taste and add more salt to the seasoning if needed. If you want the sauce to be smoother, you can strain it through a fine mesh screen.
8. Apply a coat on the wings:
9. After the wings are done, place them in a big bowl.
10. Coat the wings equally by tossing them in the mango habanero sauce.
11. Serve: Arrange the hot mango habanero chicken wings and top with chopped green onions or fresh cilantro, if you'd like.

NOTE:

➢ Start with one habanero pepper and add more to taste if you like less heat.
➢ You can incorporate some smoked paprika into the seasoning mixture to give it a smokey taste.

INGREDIENTS:

For the Chicken:

- ❖ Skinless, boneless chicken thighs or breasts, 1 pound (450 grams)
- ❖ 1 cup buttermilk
- ❖ 1 cup all-purpose flour
- ❖ 1/2 cup cornstarch
- ❖ 1/2 teaspoon paprika
- ❖ 1/2 teaspoon garlic powder
- ❖ 1/2 teaspoon onion powder
- ❖ 1/2 teaspoon dried thyme
- ❖ 1/2 teaspoon dried oregano
- ❖ 1/4 teaspoon cayenne pepper (optional for heat)
- ❖ Salt and black pepper, to taste
- ❖ Cooking spray

For the Waffles:

- ❖ 1 1/2 cups all-purpose flour
- ❖ 2 tablespoons granulated sugar
- ❖ 1 tablespoon baking powder
- ❖ 1/2 teaspoon salt
- ❖ 1 large egg
- ❖ 1 1/4 cups milk
- ❖ 1/4 cup unsalted butter, melted
- ❖ 1 teaspoon vanilla extract

For Serving:

- ❖ Maple syrup
- ❖ Butter (optional)
- ❖ Fresh fruit (optional)

INSTRUCTIONS:

1. To marinate the chicken, put the pieces of chicken in a basin and cover them with buttermilk. For optimal effects, cover and refrigerate for at least one hour, preferably overnight.
2. Mix the flour, cornstarch, paprika, onion and garlic powders, thyme, oregano, salt, black pepper, and cayenne (if using) in a large basin to prepare the Chicken Coating.
3. Coat the Chicken: Take it out of the buttermilk and let any extra runoff.
4. To make sure the chicken pieces are well coated, lightly press them after dredging them in the flour mixture.
5. Heat the Air Fryer: Set the air fryer's temperature for five minutes to 380°F (190°C).
6. To cook the chicken, lightly mist the cooking spray within the air fryer basket.
7. Put the coated chicken pieces in the basket in a single layer. Depending on how big your air fryer is, you might have to cook in batches.
8. After the chicken is thoroughly cooked and crispy, air fry it for 20 to 25 minutes, rotating it halfway through, at 380°F (190°C). Internal temperature needs to be attained at 165°F (74°C).
9. Prepare the waffles:
10. Toss the salt, baking soda, sugar, and flour in a large bowl.

11. In another bowl, stir milk, egg, melted butter, and vanillaextract.
12. Mix dry ingredients just before adding liquids. The batter will have lumps.
13. Prepare the waffles: Preheat your waffle iron according to the manufacturer's instructions.
14. If necessary, lightly oil the waffle iron.
15. Transfer the batter onto the waffle iron that has been warmed, and cook it as directed by the maker, until it turns golden brown and crisp.
16. Present: Arrange the waffles with the crispy chicken on top.
17. If preferred, top with a pat of butter and drizzle with maple syrup.
18. Garnish with fresh fruit for flavor.

NOTE:

➤ For extra flavor, add smoked paprika to the chicken coating or cinnamon to the waffle batter.
➤ To achieve a crispier texture, make sure the chicken is thoroughly coated with the flour mixture.

INGREDIENTS:

For the Chicken:

- ❖ 1-pound boneless, skinless chicken breasts or thighs
- ❖ 1 cup buttermilk
- ❖ 1 cup all-purpose flour
- ❖ 1/2 cup cornstarch
- ❖ 1 teaspoon paprika
- ❖ 1 teaspoon garlic powder
- ❖ 1 teaspoon onion powder
- ❖ 1/2 teaspoon dried oregano
- ❖ 1/2 teaspoon salt
- ❖ 1/4 teaspoon black pepper
- ❖ Cooking spray

For the Buffalo Sauce:

- ❖ 1/2 cup Frank's RedHot spicy sauce
- ❖ 1/4 cup unsalted butter
- ❖ 1 tablespoon white vinegar
- ❖ 1 tablespoon honey
- ❖ 1/4 teaspoon garlic powder

For the Sandwiches:

- ❖ 4 hamburger buns
- ❖ Lettuce leaves
- ❖ Sliced tomato
- ❖ Pickles
- ❖ Ranch or blue cheese dressing (optional)

INSTRUCTIONS:

1. To marinate the chicken, put the pieces of chicken in a basin and cover them with buttermilk. For optimal effects, cover and refrigerate for at least one hour, preferably overnight.
2. Get the coating for the chicken ready:
3. Combine the flour, cornstarch, paprika, onion and garlic powders, oregano, salt, and black pepper in a big basin.
4. Coat the Chicken: Take it out of the buttermilk and let any extra runoff.
5. To make sure the chicken pieces are well coated, lightly press them after dredging them in the flour mixture.
6. Heat the Air Fryer: Set the air fryer's temperature for five minutes to 380°F (190°C).
7. To cook the chicken, lightly mist the cooking spray within the air fryer basket.
8. Put the coated chicken pieces in a single layer of the basket. Depending on how big your air fryer is, you might have to cook in batches.
9. When the chicken is crispy and cooked through, air fry it for 18 to 20 minutes at 380°F (190°C), turning it halfway through. A temperature of 165°F (74°C) should be reached internally.
10. Get the Buffalo Sauce ready.
11. Melt the butter in a small saucepan over a medium heat.
12. Add the garlic powder, honey, white vinegar, and spicy sauce and stir. Cook the sauce until it's well mixed and heated through, stirring from time to time. Take off the heat.
13. Apply Sauce to the Chicken: After the chicken is done, move it to a big bowl.
14. After adding the buffalo sauce to the chicken, toss to cover it completely.

15. Assemble the sandwiches:
16. If preferred, lightly brown the hamburger buns in the air fryer for two to three minutes at 350°F/175°C.
17. Top each bottom half of the bread with a slice of buffalo chicken and lettuce leaves.
18. Add pickles, tomato slices, and, if like, a sprinkle of ranch or blue cheese dressing on top. Top half of bun should be placed on top.
19. Serve: Warm up the buffalo chicken sandwiches and accompany them with your preferred sides.

NOTE:

➢ Hot sauce can be added to buffalo sauce to tailor spiciness.
➢ For crunch, top the sandwich with shredded cabbage or slaw.

INGREDIENTS:

- ❖ 4 boneless, skinless chicken breasts (680 g, 1.5 lbs)
- ❖ 2 tablespoons olive oil
- ❖ 1 lemon, zest and juice
- ❖ 2 cloves garlic, minced
- ❖ 1 tablespoon fresh basil, finely chopped (or one teaspoon dried basil)
- ❖ 1 teaspoon dried oregano
- ❖ 1/2 teaspoon salt
- ❖ 1/4 teaspoon black pepper

INSTRUCTIONS:

1. To marinade chicken, mix olive oil, lemon zest, lemon juice, minced garlic, basil, oregano, salt, and black pepper in a bowl.
2. Chicken breasts should be marinated in a shallow dish or large plastic bag. For optimal flavor, cover and chill for 30 minutes or two hours.
3. Pre-heat t
4. he air fryer for five minutes at 375°F (190°C).
5. Cook Chicken: Remove chicken breasts from marinade and dry with paper towels. Discard marinade.
6. Use cooking spray lightly on the air fryer basket.
7. Single-layer the chicken breasts in the air fryer basket. Air fryers vary in size, so you may have to cook in batches.
8. Air fried the chicken for 15–18 minutes at 375°F (190°C), flipping halfway, until the internal temperature reaches 165°F (74°C).

Serve:

- ➤ Before slicing, give the chicken a few minutes to rest.
- ➤ Choose between roasted veggies, rice, or a crisp salad to go with the lemon basil chicken breasts.

NOTE:

- ➤ Add fresh basil or lemon zest to chicken before serving for flavor.
- ➤ Breadcrumbs and Parmesan cheese can be sparingly sprinkled on air-fried chicken for crunch.

INGREDIENTS:

- ❖ One pound (450 grams) of skinless, boneless chicken thighs or breasts, chopped into bite-sized pieces
- ❖ 1 tablespoon olive oil
- ❖ 1 tablespoon fajita seasoning (store-bought or homemade)
- ❖ 1/2 teaspoon garlic powder
- ❖ 1/2 teaspoon onion powder
- ❖ 1/2 teaspoon paprika
- ❖ 1/2 teaspoon dried oregano
- ❖ 1/2 teaspoon ground cumin
- ❖ 1/4 teaspoon salt
- ❖ 1/4 teaspoon black pepper

For Serving (Optional):

- ❖ Mini flour tortillas or tortilla chips
- ❖ Sour cream
- ❖ Salsa or pico de gallo
- ❖ Shredded cheese
- ❖ Sliced jalapeños
- ❖ Fresh cilantro, chopped

INSTRUCTIONS:

1. To make the chicken
2. , in a big bowl, mix together olive oil, salt, black pepper, paprika, oregano, cumin, onion powder, and garlic powder.
3. Toss the chicken pieces again to coat with the spice mixture.
4. For five minutes, heat t
5. he air fryer to 400°F (200°C).
6. Spray the air fryer basket
7. lightly before frying the chicken.
8. Place seasoned chicken pieces in the air fryer basket in a single layer. You may need to cook in batches depending on your air fryer size.
9. Shake the basket in the middle. To cook the chicken to 165°F (74°C), bake it at 400°F (200°C) for 10–12 minutes.

To serve, move the bite-sized chicken fajitas to a serving plate.

Serve with Mexican chips or tiny flour tortillas and your preferred toppings, including salsa, shredded cheese, sour cream, sliced jalapeños, and fresh cilantro.

NOTE:

➢ Before serving, pour some lime juice over the chicken for a little more flavor.
➢ For the whole fajita experience, you can, if you'd like, add sliced bell peppers and onions to the air fryer along with the chicken. After thinly slicing them, toss them with olive oil and fajita seasoning and then air-fry them.

INGREDIENTS:

For the Chicken Tenders:

- ❖ 1 lb (450 g) chicken tenders or chicken breasts cut into strips
- ❖ 1 cup buttermilk
- ❖ 1 cup all-purpose flour
- ❖ 1/2 cup cornstarch
- ❖ 1 teaspoon paprika
- ❖ 1 teaspoon garlic powder
- ❖ 1 teaspoon onion powder
- ❖ 1/2 teaspoon salt
- ❖ 1/4 teaspoon black pepper
- ❖ Cooking spray

For the Honey Sriracha Sauce:

- ❖ 1/4 cup honey
- ❖ 2 tablespoons sriracha sauce (adjust to taste for heat)
- ❖ 1 tablespoon soy sauce
- ❖ 1 tablespoon rice vinegar
- ❖ 1 teaspoon minced garlic
- ❖ 1 teaspoon grated ginger (optional)

INSTRUCTIONS:

1. Chicken should be marinated. Put the chicken tenders in a basin and cover them with buttermilk. Cover and chill for at least 30 minutes or up to 2 hours for optimal effects.

2. To make the Chicken Coating, combine the flour, cornstarch, paprika, onion and garlic powders, salt, and black pepper in a big basin.
3. To coat the chicken, take the chicken tenders from the buttermilk and let the extra runoff.
4. After dredging the chicken tenders in the flour mixture, lightly press them to ensure they are well coated.
5. Heat the Air Fryer: Set the air fryer's temperature to 380°F (190°C) for five minutes.
6. To cook the chicken tenders, lightly mist the cooking spray inside the air fryer basket.
7. Arrange the breaded chicken tenders in the basket in a single layer. Your air fryer's size will determine whether you need to cook in batches or not.
8. Air-fry the chicken tenders for 10 to 12 minutes at 380°F (190°C), flipping them halfway through, or until they are crispy and cooked through. Internal temperature needs to be attained at 165°F (74°C).
9. To make the Honey Sriracha Sauce, put the honey, soy sauce, rice vinegar, minced garlic, and grated ginger (if using) in a small pot.
10. Cook the SauceSauce over medium heat, stirring regularly, until it thickens slightly and is well-cooked. Take off the heat.
11. Apply SauceSauce to the Chicken: After the chicken tenders are done, move them to a big bowl.
12. After covering the chicken tenders with the honey-sriracha sauce, toss to ensure an even coating.

Serve warm honey-sriracha chicken tenders, and serve additional SauceSauce on the side. They go nicely with fresh salads, grains, and veggies.

NOTE:

➢ Adjust the amount of sriracha in the SauceSauce to customize the heat intensity.
➢ Before serving, add chopped green onions or sesame seeds for crispness.

INGREDIENTS:

- ❖ 4 large bell peppers (any color)
- ❖ 1 lb (450 g) cooked chicken breast or rotisserie chicken, shredded or diced
- ❖ 1 cup cooked rice or quinoa
- ❖ 1 cup Alfredo sauce (store-bought or homemade)
- ❖ 1/2 cup grated Parmesan cheese
- ❖ 1/2 cup shredded mozzarella cheese
- ❖ 1 cup baby spinach or chopped fresh spinach
- ❖ 1/2 teaspoon garlic powder
- ❖ 1/2 teaspoon dried Italian seasoning
- ❖ Salt and black pepper, to taste
- ❖ Cooking spray

INSTRUCTIONS:

1. Prepare the bell peppers by chopping off the tops and removing the membranes and seeds. Coat the peppers with a light layer of frying spray.
2. Heat the Air Fryer: Set the air fryer's temperature to 360°F (182°C) for five minutes.
3. Prepare the Filling: Combine the cooked chicken, cooked rice or quinoa, Alfredo sauce, mozzarella and Parmesan cheeses, spinach, Italian seasoning, garlic powder, and black pepper in a large bowl. Blend until thoroughly blended.
4. Stuff the Peppers: Gently stuff each bell pepper with a small amount of the chicken Alfredo mixture.

5. Cook the Stuffed Peppers: Put the stuffed peppers in the air fryer basket, standing upright. Your air fryer's size will determine whether you need to cook in batches or not.
6. Air fry the peppers for 12 to 15 minutes, or until they are soft and the filling is bubbling and well heated, at 360°F (182°C). Internally, a temperature of 165°F (74°C) should be reached.

Serve:

➢ *Before presenting, allow the filled peppers to settle for a few minutes.*
➢ *If preferred, garnish with more Parmesan cheese or finely chopped fresh parsley.*

NOTE:

➢ For the final three minutes of cooking, you can top the filling with extra mozzarella cheese if you want it crispier.
➢ You can also incorporate sauteed onions, mushrooms, or other veggies into the stuffing for added taste and nutrition.

INGREDIENTS:

For the Chicken:

- ❖ One pound (450 grams) of skinless, boneless chicken thighs or breasts, sliced into thin strips
- ❖ 1 cup buttermilk
- ❖ 1 cup all-purpose flour
- ❖ 1/2 cup cornstarch
- ❖ 1 teaspoon paprika
- ❖ 1 teaspoon garlic powder
- ❖ 1 teaspoon onion powder
- ❖ 1/2 teaspoon dried oregano
- ❖ 1/2 teaspoon ground cumin
- ❖ 1/2 teaspoon chili powder
- ❖ 1/2 teaspoon salt
- ❖ 1/4 teaspoon black pepper
- ❖ Cooking spray

For the Tacos:

- ❖ 8 small taco shells or tortillas
- ❖ 1 cup shredded lettuce
- ❖ 1 cup diced tomatoes
- ❖ 1/2 cup shredded cheddar cheese
- ❖ Half-cup Greek yogurt or sour cream
- ❖ 1/4 cup salsa or pico
- ❖ Lime wedges for serving
- ❖ Fresh cilantro, chopped (optional)

INSTRUCTIONS:

1. Prepare the chicken by putting the chicken strips in a bowl and dousing them with buttermilk. Cover and chill for at least 30 minutes or up to two hours for optimal effects.
2. To make the Chicken Coating, combine the flour, cornstarch, paprika, onion, garlic, oregano, cumin, chili powder, salt, and black pepper in a big bowl.
3. To coat the chicken, remove the buttermilk strips and let the extra runoff.
4. After dredging the chicken strips in the flour mixture, lightly press them to ensure they are well covered.
5. Heat the Air Fryer: Set the air fryer's temperature to 380°F (190°C) for five minutes.
6. To cook the chicken, lightly mist the cooking spray within the air fryer basket.
7. Put the coated chicken strips in the basket in a single layer. Depending on the size of your air fryer, you might have to cook in batches.
8. When the chicken is crispy and cooked, air fry it for 10 to 12 minutes at 380°F (190°C), turning it halfway through. Internally, it should reach 165°F (74°C).
9. As the chicken cooks, prepare the tacos by heating the tortillas or taco shells according to the package directions.
10. When the chicken is done, could you put it on a platter?
11. Put the Tacos together:
12. Top each taco shell or tortilla with a couple of crispy chicken pieces, chopped tomatoes, and shredded lettuce.
13. Add Greek yogurt or sour cream, salsa, pico de gallo, and grated cheddar.

Serve:

> ➤ If wanted, garnish with lime wedges and fresh cilantro.
> ➤ While the chicken is still warm, serve the crispy chicken tacos immediately.

NOTE:

> ➤ Add more taco toppings, such as chopped red onions, avocado, and sliced jalapeños.
> ➤ Before adding the sour cream or Greek yogurt to the tacos, stir in hot sauce for an extra spicy bite.

INGREDIENTS:

- ❖ 2 lbs (900 g) chicken wings, separated into drumettes and flats
- ❖ 1 cup plain yogurt (Greek yogurt works well)
- ❖ 2 tablespoons tandoori spice mix (store-bought or homemade)
- ❖ 1 tablespoon lemon juice
- ❖ 1 tablespoon vegetable oil
- ❖ 1 teaspoon garlic powder
- ❖ 1 teaspoon ginger powder
- ❖ 1/2 teaspoon paprika
- ❖ 1/2 teaspoon ground turmeric
- ❖ 1/2 teaspoon ground cumin
- ❖ 1/2 teaspoon ground coriander
- ❖ 1/2 teaspoon salt
- ❖ 1/4 teaspoon black pepper

INSTRUCTIONS:

1. To marinate the chicken wings, combine the yogurt, tandoori spice mix, lemon juice, vegetable oil, paprika, turmeric, cumin, coriander, salt, and black pepper in a large bowl.
2. After adding the chicken wings to the dish, toss them around to ensure the marinade coats them evenly.
3. Cover the bowl and place it in the refrigerator for at least one hour or up to overnightfor the best flavor.
4. To warm up the air fryer, adjust the temperature to 380°F (190°C) for five minutes.

5. Before you fry the chicken wings, lightly sprinkle the cooking spray within the air fryer basket.
6. Arrange the marinated chicken wings within the basket in a single layer. Depending on how big your air fryer is, you might have to cook in batches.
7. Bake the chicken wings at 380°F (190°C) for 20 to 25 minutes, rotating them halfway through, or until they are cooked through and crispy. It is necessary to reach an internal temperature of 165°F (74°C).

To serve, move the chicken wings with tandoori sauce onto a serving plate.

Accompany with a crisp salad, naan bread, or a chilled cucumber raita.

NOTE:

➢ To customize the heat level of the wings, adjust the quantity of tandoori spice mix used.
➢ Before serving, top the wings with a squeeze of lemon juice and some fresh cilantro for a more genuine look.

INGREDIENTS:

- ❖ 4 skinless, boneless chicken breasts, 680 g (1.5 lbs)
- ❖ 1 cup of 2% or full-fat plain Greek yogurt
- ❖ 2 tablespoons olive oil
- ❖ 2 tablespoons lemon juice
- ❖ 3 cloves garlic, minced
- ❖ 1 tablespoon dried oregano
- ❖ 1 teaspoon dried thyme
- ❖ 1 teaspoon paprika
- ❖ 1/2 teaspoon ground cumin
- ❖ 1/2 teaspoon salt
- ❖ 1/4 teaspoon black pepper
- ❖ Fresh parsley, chopped (optional, for garnish)

INSTRUCTIONS:

1. Marinade ingredients include Greek yogurt, olive oil, lemon juice, cumin, paprika, oregano, black pepper, and chopped garlic. Combine all of these ingredients in a big basin.
2. Chicken needs to be marinated. Place the chicken breasts in a basin and brush both sides with marinade.
3. For optimal flavor, cover and let sit for at least one hour, but preferably up to four hours.full-fat
4. The air fryer needs five minutes of preheating at 375°F, or 190°C.
5. Season the chicken with a little cooking spray and place it in the air fryer basket.

6. The chicken breasts should be drained of any excess marinade.
7. Make sure the
8. re's only one layer of chicken breasts in the air fryer basket. Your air fryer's capacity will determine how many batchesyou'll need to cook at once.
9. The chicken should be air-fried for 15 to 18 minutes at 375°F (190°C), turning once halfway through, or until it reaches an internal temperature of 165°F (74°C).

After letting the chicken breasts rest for a few minutes, slice them and serve.

Toss with some fresh parsley and enjoy with some roasted veggies, rice, or a refreshing salad.

NOTE:

➢ Before serving, give the chicken a last sprinkling of lemon zest for more flavor.
➢ If you like your pizza a little crunchier, sprinkle the outside with a thin layer of breadcrumbs flavored with Parmesan cheese before air-frying.

INGREDIENTS:

- ❖ thinly sliced, boneless, skinless chicken breasts, 1 pound (450 grams)
- ❖ 4 large flour tortillas or wraps
- ❖ 6 slices bacon, cooked and crumbled
- ❖ 1 cup shredded cheddar cheese
- ❖ 1 cup ranch dressing
- ❖ 1 cup baby spinach or shredded lettuce
- ❖ 1 cup diced tomatoes
- ❖ 1/2 teaspoon garlic powder
- ❖ 1/2 teaspoon onion powder
- ❖ 1/2 teaspoon paprika
- ❖ 1/2 teaspoon dried oregano
- ❖ Salt and black pepper, to taste
- ❖ Cooking spray

INSTRUCTIONS:

1. To make the chicken
2. , put the paprika, onion powder, oregano, salt, black pepper, and garlic powder in a bowl.
3. Toss the chicken strips with the spice mixtureafter they have been thoroughly coated.
4. Five minutes in advance, set the air fryer's temperature to 380°F, or 190°C. The chicken needs to be cooked next.
5. Cooking spray should only be used sparingly on the air fryer basket.

6. Arrange the spice-coated chicken pieces in the basket in a single layer. In case the air fryer is small, you might have to cook in batches.
7. Shake the basket after 8 to 10 minutes of air fry time at 380°F (190°C), or until the chicken achieves an internal temperature of 165°F (74°C).
8. Put the Wraps Together: While the chicken cooks, warm the tortillas according to the package's instructions.
9. Top each tortilla with a dollop of ranch dressing.
10. Add cooked chicken strips, diced tomatoes, shredded cheddar cheese, crumbled bacon, and baby spinach or shredded lettuce.
11. To wrap and toast, carefully roll each tortilla around the filling.
12. Use cooking spray sparingly on the wraps' exteriors.
13. Spoon the wraps into the air fryer basket, seam side down. Depending on the size of your air fryer, you might have to cook in batches.
14. The wraps should be air-fried for 4–6 minutes at 375°F (190°C), turning halfway through or until the cheese is melted and crispy.

Serve:

➢ *Halve the wraps and present them warm, accompanied by an additional ranch dressing or your preferred dipping sauce.*

NOTE:

➢ Before rolling, add thinly sliced bell peppers or red onions to the wraps for some crunch.
➢ If preferred, you can use your preferred dressing or SauceSauce in place of the ranch dressing.

INGREDIENTS:

- ❖ 4 bone-in, skinless chicken thighs (about 1.5 lbs or 680 g)
- ❖ 3 tablespoons unsalted butter, melted
- ❖ 4 cloves garlic, minced
- ❖ 1 tablespoon olive oil
- ❖ 1 tablespoon of minced parsley, either fresh or dried
- ❖ 1 teaspoon dried thyme
- ❖ 1 teaspoon paprika
- ❖ 1/2 teaspoon onion powder
- ❖ 1/2 teaspoon garlic powder
- ❖ 1/2 teaspoon salt
- ❖ 1/4 teaspoon black pepper

INSTRUCTIONS:

1. Dissolve garlic powder in a single basin and combine with paprika, lemon juice, black pepper, and parsley. Combine olive oil, garlic powder, and lemon juice in an additional basin. Butter should be prepared.
2. Complete the poultry and arrange it on a plate. Utilize paper towels to dry poultry t-dabs.
3. Before serving, apply garlic butter to the chicken thighs.
4. Before utilizing the air fryer, allow it to reach a temperature of 450°F for five minutes. The optimal temperature is 380°F (190°C).
5. Before adding the poultry to the air fryer basket, grease it.
6. Compact air fryers cook. Air-fry
7. chicken legs skin-side down.

8. After 18–22 minutes, turn chicken. Stay at 190°C (165°F) for an hour. Solid, rich dark skin is good.

Serve:

➢ Before serving, give the chicken thighs a few minutes to rest.
➢ Add more chopped parsley to the garnish and serve with roasted vegetables, rice, or a crisp salad as a side.

NOTE:

➢ Before serving, pour some lemon juice over the chicken thighs for more flavor.
➢ Add one more minced garlic clove to the butter mixture for a more pungent garlic taste.

96. BBQ CHICKEN QUESADILLAS

INGREDIENTS:

- ❖ Two cups either chopped or shredded cooked chicken breast or rotisserie chicken.
- ❖ 1/2 cup BBQ sauce (your favorite brand or homemade)
- ❖ 1 cup shredded cheddar cheese
- ❖ 1 cup shredded mozzarella cheese
- ❖ 4 large flour tortillas
- ❖ One half cup finely sliced red onion (optional)
- ❖ 1/2 cup sliced bell peppers (optional)
- ❖ 1 tablespoon olive oil
- ❖ Cooking spray

INSTRUCTIONS:

1. To make the chicken filling, combine the shredded chicken and BBQ sauce, stirring to coat the chicken thoroughly.
2. Place one tortilla on a level surface to assemble the quesadillas.
3. Evenly distribute half of the mozzarella and cheddar cheeses on top of the tortilla.
4. Over the cheese, distribute half of the BBQ chicken mixture.
5. If using, Top the chicken with thinly sliced bell peppers and red onions.
6. Add a small amount of cheese to the chicken and vegetables.
7. Top with another tortilla to enclose the filling.
8. Five minutes of preheating at 375°F (190°C)

9. should be used to get the air fryer ready.
10. Air fryer quesadillas require shaking the frying spray with water.
11. Place quesadilla in air fryer. It depends on your air fryer size.
12. Add olive oil to a tortilla.
13. Bake the quesadilla at 375°F (190°C) for 6–8 minutes until the cheese melts and the tortilla is crispy and golden brown. It needs one turn.
14. Allow air-fried quesadillas to cool for 1 minute. Finally, cut everything.As an appetizer, serve with guacamole, salsa, or sour cream.
15. Slice it and serve with salsa, sour cream, or guacamole.

NOTE:

➢ To increase the heat of the BBQ chicken mixture, you may incorporate sliced jalapeños or a sprinkling of red pepper flakes.
➢ You can increase the flavor factor of the filling by including some sautéed spinach or mushrooms.

INGREDIENTS:

For the Chicken Wings:

- ❖ 2 lbs (900 g) chicken wings, separated into drumettes and flats
- ❖ 1 tablespoon vegetable oil
- ❖ 1/2 teaspoon garlic powder
- ❖ 1/2 teaspoon onion powder
- ❖ 1/2 teaspoon ground ginger
- ❖ 1/4 teaspoon salt
- ❖ 1/4 teaspoon black pepper

For the Asian Glaze:

- ❖ 1/4 cup soy sauce
- ❖ 1/4 cup hoisin sauce
- ❖ 2 tablespoons honey
- ❖ 2 tablespoons rice vinegar
- ❖ 1 tablespoon sesame oil
- ❖ 2 cloves garlic, minced
- ❖ 1 teaspoon fresh ginger, grated
- ❖ One tablespoon of water and one teaspoon of cornstarch (optional thickening)

INSTRUCTIONS:

1. The chicken wings should be prepared by patting them dry with paper towels.
2. After being tossed in a big basin with vegetable oil, ground ginger, onion powder, garlic powder, and black pepper, the chicken wings should be equally coated.
3. Heat the Air Fryer: Set the air fryer's temperature to 380°F (190°C) for five minutes.
4. To cook the chicken wings, lightly mist the cooking spray within the air fryer basket.
5. Simmer until the glaze thickens, one to two more minutes. Turn off the heat.
6. Once cooked, transfer the glaze from the chicken wings into a large basin.
7. Pour the
8. Asian glaze over the wings and toss to fully coat.

Serve:

➢ Add sesame seeds and chopped green onions as garnish, if you'd like.
➢ Serve warm Asian-glazed chicken wings over steamed rice or alongside a crisp salad, depending on your tastes.

NOTE:

➢ Before serving, top the glazed wings with chopped cilantro and more sesame seeds for added flavor.
➢ You can adjust the amount of honey or soy sauce to suit your taste and change the glaze's sweetness or saltiness.

INGREDIENTS:

- ❖ One pound (450 grams) of skinless, boneless chicken thighs or breasts, chopped into bite-sized pieces

For the Marinade:

- ❖ 1/4 cup plain Greek yogurt
- ❖ 2 tablespoons olive oil
- ❖ 2 tablespoons lemon juice
- ❖ 3 cloves garlic, minced
- ❖ 1 tablespoon ground cumin
- ❖ 1 tablespoon ground paprika
- ❖ 1 teaspoon ground turmeric
- ❖ 1 teaspoon ground coriander
- ❖ 1 teaspoon ground cinnamon
- ❖ 1/2 teaspoon ground allspice
- ❖ 1/2 teaspoon ground black pepper
- ❖ 1/2 teaspoon salt
- ❖ 1/4 teaspoon cayenne pepper (optional, for extra heat)

For Serving:

- ❖ Pita bread or flatbread
- ❖ Hummus or tzatziki sauce
- ❖ Fresh vegetables like cucumber, tomatoes, and red onions
- ❖ Fresh parsley or cilantro, chopped (optional)

INSTRUCTIONS:

1. Greek yogurt, olive oil, lemon juice, minced garlic, cumin, paprika, turmeric, coriander, cinnamon, allspice, black pepper, salt, and cayenne pepper (if using) should all be combined in a big basin to marinate the chicken.
2. When the chicken pieces are added, toss them to coat them equally with marinade.
3. For a stronger flavor, cover and refrigerate for an hour or overnight.
4. To warm up the air fryer, adjust the temperature to 380°F (190°C) for five minutes.
5. Before frying the chicken shawarma bits, lightly mist the air fryer basket with cooking spray.
6. Put the chicken pieces that have been marinated in a single layer inside the basket. Depending on how big your air fryer is, you might have to cook in batches.
7. When the air fry cycle reaches 12 to 15 minutes at 380°F (190°C), or when the chicken is cooked through and the internal temperature reaches 165°F (74°C), shake the basket halfway through. The chicken should be well-browned throughout with perfectly crispy edges.

Serve:

➤ If preferred, reheat the flatbreads or pita bread.
➤ Present the mini chicken shawarma pieces alongside fresh veggies such tomatoes, cucumbers, and red onions, as well as tzatziki or hummus sauce.
➤ If desired, sprinkle with chopped cilantro or parsley.

NOTE:

➢ For extra flavor, you may serve the shawarma pieces with a drizzle of tahini sauce or a squeeze of lemon juice.
➢ A simple salad with fresh vegetables and some marinade also makes a great side dish.

INGREDIENTS:

For the Potatoes:

- ❖ 4 large russet potatoes
- ❖ Olive oil
- ❖ Salt and pepper

For the Filling:

- ❖ One cup of rotisserie chicken or chicken breast that has been cooked, diced, or shredded
- ❖ One cup of broccoli florets, boiled and chopped
- ❖ A half-cup of cheddar cheese, shredded
- ❖ 1/4 cup sour cream, Greek yogurt, or both
- ❖ a quarter cup of milk
- ❖ 2 tablespoons butter
- ❖ 1/2 teaspoon garlic powder
- ❖ 1/2 teaspoon onion powder
- ❖ 1/4 teaspoon paprika
- ❖ 1/4 teaspoon salt
- ❖ 1/4 teaspoon black pepper

INSTRUCTIONS:

1. Wash and scrape the potatoes to prepare them. Using paper towels, pat dry the areas.
2. Season with salt and pepper after giving each potato a quick olive oil rub.
3. Make several piercings in each potato with a fork.

4. Before cooking the potatoes, preheat the air fryer for five minutes to 400°F (200°C).
5. Place the potatoes in the air fryer basket in a single layer. The necessity of batch cooking will depend on the size of your air fryer.
6. Warm up the oven to 200°C, or 400°F. After 20 to 25 minutes of baking, flip the potatoes halfway through.
7. In a big bowl, mix together the shredded chicken, chopped broccoli, grated cheddar cheese, sour cream or Greek yogurt, milk, butter, paprika, onion powder, garlic powder, and black pepper to make the filling while the potatoes are cooking. Blend until well combined.
8. After cooking, carefully cut the potatoes open lengthwise, leaving a pocket in the center, and stuff.
9. To make a bit more space for the filling, gently fluff the insides of the potatoes with a fork.
10. To distribute the chicken and broccoli mixture evenly among the potatoes, spoon into the potato pockets.
11. To complete cooking, move the stuffed potatoes around in the air fryer basket.
12. Bake at 400°F (200°C) for 5 to 7 minutes, or until the cheese is bubbling and melted and the filling is heated through.

To serve, take the stuffed potatoes out of the air fryer and allow them to cool a little.

NOTE:

- ➢ Before the last cooking stage, you can add more shredded cheese to the filling for taste.
- ➢ For even more freshness, you can garnish with fresh herbs like chives or parsley.

INGREDIENTS:

- ❖ 1 lb (450 g) chicken tenders
- ❖ 1 cup cream cheese, softened
- ❖ 1/2 cup shredded cheddar cheese
- ❖ 1/4 cup crumbled bacon (cooked)
- ❖ 2-3 fresh jalapeños, finely diced (remove seeds for less heat)
- ❖ 1/2 teaspoon garlic powder
- ❖ 1/4 teaspoon onion powder
- ❖ 1/4 teaspoon smoked paprika
- ❖ Salt and black pepper, to taste
- ❖ 1 cup all-purpose flour
- ❖ 2 large eggs, beaten
- ❖ 1 1/2 cups panko breadcrumbs
- ❖ Cooking spray

INSTRUCTIONS:

1. Mix cream cheese, shredded cheddar cheese, bacon, chopped jalapeños, smoked paprika, onion powder, garlic powder, and black pepper in a medium-sized bowl to make the filling. Blend until thoroughly blended.
2. Carefully cut a small slit on the side of each chicken tender to form a pocket before stuffing them. Take care to avoid slicing through completely.
3. Scoop the jalapeño popper filling into each pocket. If necessary, secure the opening with toothpicks.
4. Bread the chicken tenders at a breading station by arranging three shallow dishes—one containing flour,

another containing beaten eggs, and a third containing panko breadcrumbs.

5. Shake off excess flour after dredging each filled chicken tender in flour.
6. Dredge in the whisked eggs, letting the extra runoff.
7. Sprinkle with panko breadcrumbs and gently press to coat.
8. For five minutes, the air fryer needs to be warmed to 375°F (190°C).
9. Before putting the chicken tenders in the air fryer basket to fry, lightly coat them with cooking spray.
10. Arrange
11. the breaded chicken tenders in a single layer within the basket. The necessity of batch cooking will depend on the size of your air fryer.
12. Lightly coat the tops of the chicken tenders with cooking spray.
13. It takes the air fryer ten to twelve minutes to reach a temperature of 190°C, or 375°F. Once the breading is crunchy and golden brown, turn the chicken halfway through and continue cooking. It is necessary to obtain an interior temperature of 165°F (74°C).

To serve, take the chicken tenders from the air fryer and give them time to settle.

Savor with your favorite dipping sauce, such blue cheese or ranch!

NOTE:

- ➢ If you like your kick hotter, add a splash of hot sauce or leave some jalapeño seeds in the filling.
- ➢ You can incorporate some grated Parmesan cheese with the panko breadcrumbs to give them more crunch.

CONCLUSION:

The End of Your Air Fryer Journey, but Only the Beginning

Congratulations on completing your journey through "Air Fryer Magic: 100 Easy and Delicious Recipes." This culinary adventure has taken you from breakfast to dessert, exploring the air fryer's possibilities. We hope you have discovered new recipes and a newfound appreciation for the versatility, convenience, and health benefits of air frying.

Embracing a Healthier Lifestyle

One of the most significant advantages of using an air fryer is enjoying your favorite foods with less oil and fewer calories. By now, you've likely experienced how easy it is to prepare crispy, delicious meals that are both satisfying and better for your overall well-being. Whether you've made crispy chicken wings, perfectly roasted vegetables, or indulgent desserts, you've seen firsthand how the air fryer can transform everyday ingredients into culinary delights.

Healthy eating doesn't have to be about restriction or compromise. With the air fryer, you can have the best of both worlds: delicious food that's also good for you. Remember the tips and techniques you've learned as you continue to experiment and explore. Keep preheating your air fryer, avoiding overcrowding, and experimenting with flavors. These small steps make a big difference in the quality of your meals.

Expanding Your Culinary Horizons

This book aims to show you that the air fryer is much more than a device for frying. It's a tool that can help you bake, roast, grill, and even dehydrate various foods. The recipes have taken you around the globe, from American classics to international delights, showcasing the air fryer's ability to handle diverse cuisines and cooking styles.

As you grow more comfortable with your air fryer, don't hesitate to leave your comfort zone. Try new ingredients, test different cooking methods, and adapt recipes to suit your taste. The air fryer is a gateway to kitchen creativity; the more you use it, the more inventive you will become.

The Joy of Sharing

One of the most rewarding aspects of cooking is sharing your creations-with-others.
Whether it's for a special event, a casual get-
together with friends, or a family dinner, food has a remarkable ability to bring people together.The recipes in this book are designed to be shared, enjoyed, and celebrated. As you recreate these dishes, you'll make memories and create experiencesmake memories and create experiences beyond the plate.

Sustainability and Mindfulness

The air fryer also encourages a more sustainable approach to cooking. Reducing the need for excessive oil helps minimize waste and promotes healthier eating habits. Additionally, the air fryer's energy-efficient design can lead to lower electricity usage than traditional ovens, contributing to a more environmentally friendly kitchen.

Mindful cooking and eating are about appreciating the process and the results. As you continue to use your air fryer, please take a moment to consider where your ingredients come from, how they're prepared, and the joy they bring to your table. This mindful approach can enhance your cooking experience and deepen your connection to the food you eat.

Your Next Steps

Now that you've mastered a wide range of air fryer recipes, the next step is entirely up to you. Here are a few ideas to keep the momentum going:

Create Your Recipes: Use the techniques and tips you've learned to-develop-your-air-fryer-recipes.
To make recipes that are truly your own, experiment with different flavors and ingredient combinations. Throw an Air fryer Party to celebrate your newly discovered talents with the people you love.
Create a variety of appetizers, entrées, and desserts from this book to highlight the air fryer's versatility.

Explore Advanced Techniques: If you're feeling adventurous, delve deeper into advanced air frying techniques. Try sous-vide cooking followed by air frying, or explore dehydrating fruits and vegetables for healthy snacks.

Keep Learning:
Keep abreast on the most recent developments and trends in air fryer technology.
To increase your culinary knowledge, take part in cooking lessons, subscribe to food blogs, and join online cooking communities.

Final Thoughts

"Air Fryer Magic: 100 Easy and Delicious Recipes" has been a labor of love, crafted to make your cooking experience enjoyable, healthy, and innovative. Amelia Rose Garcia, with his extensive culinary expertise and passion for home cooking, hopes this book has inspired you to embrace the magic of air frying.

As you close this book, remember that the journey doesn't end here. Cooking is a continuous learning experience filled with opportunities to grow, experiment, and savor the joys of food. Your air fryer is a powerful tool, ready to assist you in creating countless more delicious meals.

Thank you for allowing this book to be a part of your culinary journey. May your air fryer continue to bring magic to your kitchen, filling your home with the irresistible aromas and flavors of homemade goodness.

Happy cooking, and bon appétit!

THE END

Made in the USA
Columbia, SC
04 September 2024

41578022R00130